For the past fifteen years, I have researched, experienced, shared, discovered and taught the power of passion. Nik Halik's book is a beautiful and inspirational example of 'passion in action'. If you have not yet discovered what your passion is, or how it could be possible for you to pursue it, then this book will be a magnificent resource. Passion in my definition is a source of 'unlimited energy from your soul, your spirit, your heart', and Nik wisely and practically shows you how and why it is necessary to overcome the fears from your mind that block you from pursuing your passion.

I agree with Nik: you have been designed by God, by the Universe, by whatever force you acknowledge, to pursue your passions with passion. The Thrillionaire® will 'thrill you to bits'! Read it, absorb it, and burst out of any of your 'mind-imposed' limits.

Charles Kovess, *Australasia's Passion Provocateur*

THE THRILLIONAIRE®

The Thrillionaire® is dedicated to my father

Konstantinos Halikopoulos.

1930 – 1993

Nik Halik

THE THRILLIONAIRE®

Make your life an epic and extraordinary adventure

Foreword by Bob Proctor

First published in Australia in 2008 by
New Holland Publishers (Australia) Pty Ltd
Sydney • Auckland • London • Cape Town

1/66 Gibbes St Chatswood NSW 2067 Australia
218 Lake Road Northcote Auckland New Zealand
86 Edgware Road London W2 2EA United Kingdom
80 McKenzie Street Cape Town 8001 South Africa

A record of this title is available from the National Library of Australia

Publisher: Fiona Schultz
Designer: Allan Cornwell
Production Controller: Linda Bottari
Printer: Ligare Book Printers, Sydney, Australia

10 9 8 7 6 5 4 3 2 1

Produced for New Holland by
Pennon Publishing
www.pennon.com.au

Acknowledgments

As I begin to reflect on the magnitude of this project, I often think back on the chapters that were written in exotic locations across the planet. Most of the writing was undertaken in the Great Pyramid of Giza, on the balcony of my cabin sailing down the Nile River in ancient Egypt or on a yacht sailing in the Greek islands of the Mediterranean. Others were written whilst living on a military base in Russia at the world's leading training facility for orbital space missions, in a storm-chasing vehicle in the heartland of America fleeing the path and destruction of menacing tornadoes or on a private scientific research vessel in the remote and pristine wilderness of the Antarctic Peninsula with its unspoilt frontier, considered to be the most beautiful place on earth.

With regards to my journey so far in life, there are quite a few individuals I would dearly love to thank. Firstly, my mother Dionisia for providing so much support and love for me. You always believed in me and exhibited incredible determination throughout my life. You are the foundation of the family and your love for us all is our strength. My sister Victoria for your twenty-four-hour-a-day commitment and unconditional support. Your constant commitment to selfless contribution makes an incredible difference. To my sister Georgia for your humour and wit and my brother Jim for your heart of gold and ever-increasing respect. To my nephews Kosta, Oscar, Dion and Felix, dream big and live with passion.

To my good friend, Bob Proctor for your wisdom, dedication to the personal development industry and for instilling in me the belief that we were all born rich. Also to Brian James, Bev Friend and Neil Kearney for being such outstanding examples of integrity and compassion for inspiring me to write *The Thrillionaire*®, I thank you for your promotional, media and publicity expertise. Also to all the staff of Pennon Publishing and New Holland Publishing, thank you for your faith in me.

To my incredible and phenomenal team of loyal partners, associates and team leaders in my global group of companies who maintained the integrity of the vision to transform lives across the globe. You tirelessly followed me around the world, at all times nurturing and cultivating client relationships and remaining supportive. Thank you for your inspirational dedication, passion, commitment and respect. A great deal of gratitude to Wolfgang, Claude, Renee, Amanda, Janet, Ben, Warren and Grace Black, Financial Freedom Institute, Adventure Odyssey®, The Intelligence Group and Web Business Institute team for your on-going commitment to excellence.

To all my clients who have attended my events and seminars worldwide, I acknowledge you for your participation and the fact you took massive action. For all the logistics staff who have assisted with the running of our Mind and Wealth Prosperity events in over five continents, thank you for your enthusiasm and support.

To the 'Ice Man' Peter Bland, Johnny Wimbrey, Matt Morris, Tony Michael, Eric Anderson and Richard Garriott for your friendship and inspiration. You all have a fascinating story and I cherish our friendship. A special thanks to the boys from Big Deal past and present. Those were some fun touring years in the music industry. In fact I am still laughing.

And finally, thank you to the Panos family, my adopted family in the United States. You were a beacon of light for me when I relocated to Los Angeles in my late teens. Also to my many friends and relations across the globe, I cherish and respect our associations. You are all incredibly unique in my life.

To the giants whose shoulders I stand upon, the mentors who have shaped my life, philosophy, wisdom and unwavering determination, I acknowledge you in *The Thrillionaire®* and salute you.

Contents

Foreword

WE HEAR A LOT OF TALK TODAY ABOUT MILLIONAIRES and billionaires, but never before have I seen the word 'Thrillionaire®'. However, it fits Nik Halik to a tee.

I have worked in the personal development industry for close to forty years. I have travelled to numerous countries and have worked in as many cultures and there are any number of people who give our program credit for becoming millionaires. I am flattered that Nik has endorsed my company's 'Born Rich' program and credits it with inspiring him to accomplish the phenomenal feats that have taken him to outer space and to the depths of the ocean. But Nik is the first one to give us credit for him becoming a Thrillionaire®. I love the word!

Directly behind my desk I have the *New Lexicon Webster's* dictionary. In it, I have found the word thrill and thriller but nowhere in the dictionary have I found the word Thrillionaire®. Not only does Nik Halik travel to places no one has ever been before, he's creating words that no one has ever heard before. But again, that fits Nik Halik to a tee. He's an extraordinary individual and his uniqueness comes out at you from every page in this book.

In the very early part of the book, Nik quotes J Paul Getty where Getty shared some fantastic advice, 'When eighty per cent of the newspaper sentiment is saying to buy, you should sell. Equally, when eighty per cent of the newspaper sentiment is saying to sell, you should buy.' Getty was, at one time, the wealthiest man in the world. Nik Halik knows where to go for advice. And, if and when he does follow someone else's advice, he makes sure the person has done what they're telling him to do. He took Getty's advice seriously and became a very wealthy man. But, as I've already mentioned, Nik is unique: he is definitely a unique individual who cuts his own path. He doesn't even follow that small percentage of the population who has created wealth. Nik is not fascinated with cars, planes and homes. He wants to use the money he has created to serve him in fulfilling his deep desires.

As you go from page to page, from story to story, you're going to be shaking your head wondering how this man developed such an extraordinary personality. He definitely is a Thrillionaire® and an excellent writer indeed. Nowhere in the book are you going to be left bored, the way he puts the words together, he paints beautiful pictures in your mind and does, in fact, take you on his journeys with him. You'll quickly see this man is in excellent physical shape, or he would never be able to accomplish what he has accomplished or what he plans to accomplish on a normal diet or exercise program.

I have a magnificent library of over 3,000 books. I can assure you Nik Halik's *The Thrillionaire®* will sit in a favourite place. As you journey through these pages, try and remember that each fascinating journey Nik has gone on was the result of a decision he made to improve the quality of his life. These decisions are definitely bringing his God-given potential to the surface. I once read where George Bernard Shaw stated that when he died, he wanted to be thoroughly used up. It is my opinion that Nik Halik subscribes to that sentiment.

It would not be difficult for me to continue writing paragraph after paragraph, praising this extraordinary man, his accomplishments in this book. However I feel it's time for you to dig into it yourself. Get a comfortable place to sit and make certain that you have the time to keep reading, as you will not want to lay this book down. And, if you have a very dear friend who you enjoy sharing things of value with, you should definitely give them a copy of *The Thrillionaire®*.

Bob Proctor

Best-selling author of *You Were Born Rich*

Introduction

A journey of a thousand miles begins with a single step – Lao Tzu

IN AN AGE WITH SO MANY DISTRACTIONS VYING FOR OUR ATTENTION, simply by reading *The Thrillionaire®* you are demonstrating your commitment to taking the inaugural step in setting yourself apart from the masses. No matter what a person's status or level of achievement in society, those who have reached a pinnacle of success in life do not rest on their laurels. No person can become so astute in any mental faculty, that they are not able to further raise their level of awareness.

The universe cannot put good into your hands until you let go of what you are holding in them. The most powerful prosperity tool is wisdom and by increasing it, your wisdom will always manifest a corresponding compounding increase in wealth. Hence, we are born to evolve and thrive on change in order to harness new energies and opportunities.

The Thrillionaire® will communicate to your inner emotions and stir the fires of your soul. It will enrich your life and guide you to the keys of Mind and Wealth Prosperity. You now hold within yourself this principle of power that contains the solutions to a brighter future, a path to greatness and the formula for reaching your peak potential. With the absolute awakening of this principle, your mental faculties will be intelligently sculptured and coherently aligned towards infinite greatness.

Today is a good day. Your dream has never been closer than it is at this exact instant. You will vividly visualise the image of what you desire in your mind. As you plant the seeds for your future prosperity, the words you speak will reflect the prosperity consciousness you possess. This discovery of your true assignment will allow the universe to provide to you your next assignment when you are overqualified for this one. Your beliefs will change as you will allow yourself the luxury of critical thinking. Like writing a movie script of your vision, you will be involving all of your senses. You will ascertain that your mind is an instrument for poverty or prosperity. This transformation of thought process will bypass your conscious resistance and connect you to the deeper levels of your emotions.

In summary, my illumination is that you will draw a line in the sand and integrate your newly inspired internal representation of core beliefs. You will have the assignment of opportunity to re-program the most powerful computer in the world – your mind, to become prosperous. Understanding that the mind is not an object but merely an activity, your mind will develop into an 'image maker' governed by universal law. I encourage you to subscribe to, enrol and nurture others into your newly discovered vision, where dreams become reality. In the end it just comes down to one thing. You can't run from the wind. You face reality. You face the world. Untie the mooring lines of limiting beliefs that hold you back from success. You trim your sails and maintain momentum. I encourage you to set sail on a voyage of evolution. I look forward to greeting you on the other side.

Live with passion and dare to dream. Make your life an epic extraordinary adventure.

Yours in prosperity,

Nik Halik

Chapter 1

The Thrillionaire®

Do not go where the path may lead, go instead where there is no path and leave a trail – Ralph Waldo Emerson

My cell phone rang, and calling me was a producer from the British production company making the television program *Lifestyles of the Rich and Famous* for European and North American viewers. He had heard about my investment exploits, my obsession with extreme adventures and how I'd literally go to the ends of the earth to fulfil my dreams. The call was early 2007, and the producer was eager to film a segment with me for the international program. He just needed to establish exactly what possessions they could film. First up, he asked me what cars I owned.

I was a bit slow answering, so he started to quote the names of the most exotic brands.

'Lamborghini or Ferrari?' he asked.

I was still thinking of what to say.

'Okay, Mercedes?'

'Well, not exactly …' I answered.

'I get it,' he went on, 'you're a Porsche man.'

'Not quite.'

'So, you're a James Bond kind of guy. You like action. I bet you've got an Aston Martin locked away.'

'Oh, I do like Aston Martins,' I replied. 'But no, I don't have one in the garage. Actually, I don't own a car.'

The telephone line seemed to go dead for a few seconds.

'Aah, you're a boat man,' the producer spouted optimistically. 'You're a sailor?'

I felt a bit embarrassed. 'I like yachting, yes, but, I'm sorry, I don't have a yacht either.'

He was speechless.

I explained to him that my golden rule thus far was to not invest in anything that moves, and that's why I didn't have a car, a boat or even works of art. I then enlightened him that with regards to investing, for the last eighteen years I have aggressively subscribed to an *asset accumulation* and *compounding regime* of my life and have not entertained the idea of purchasing liabilities that depreciated.

It is alleged that Albert Einstein, arguably one of the most intelligent people who ever lived, was asked what he thought was the greatest of mankind's discoveries. His candid answer is also alleged to have been: 'compound interest', the *eighth wonder of the world* and 'the greatest mathematical discovery of all time.' I provided this insight to the producer that to be a successful investor, it is important to understand the laws that govern investment growth and the mathematical laws of how compounded money really grows.

The producer decided that they would proceed with the filming anyway, no doubt assuming that they'd get plenty of interesting footage out of my asset-rich business portfolio and a preview of my thrill seeking adventures. I make no apology for not fitting the stereotype of a person who has wealth and the trappings of it. Most people equate wealth with the trappings, the luxury items and opulence. I'm not into any of that. I guess I come from outside the square. People have this stereotypical view that wealthy people should be glamorous. The glamour aspect doesn't grab me. I've always believed that wealth isn't just about what you can buy. Wealth is a like a four-legged table. The monetary aspect is just one leg. The other quadrant legs include emotional wealth, spiritual wealth and physical wealth.

Real wealth is having an abundance of ideas and a strong belief system which underpins everything you do in life. Ninety-nine per cent of what I consider to be wealth is derived from one's belief system. The monetary strategies to become financially abundant comprise just one per cent of the equation. I recall my earlier life which was more money focused and orientated, whereas these days I am more cause orientated. In life there is no sense in possessing great financial wealth and not being happy. Equally, there's no point in being rich and being physically unwell.

Individuals who seek status symbols in life have a fixation on synthetic wealth, because they need something to reassure them artificially so they can impress others they don't particularly like. I am the type of personality to save, invest and attain self-mastery for the long term, rather than some people who blow their cash on Ferraris and young third wives. People should feel good about themselves because of what they are, and what they do – not what they have in their garage.

But, as I said, I don't consider things that move to be an investment. My number one rule in an *Accumulation Asset Phase®* of one's life is to not invest in anything that moves, unless you have a validated reason. Can you name something that appreciates in value that moves? An automotive will need to be a classic vintage in order for it to appreciate. The mandatory rule is that you adequately furnish your mind and ensure your financial foundation has been solidified and primed to erect your skyscraper and monument to your existence. Welcome to Financial Prosperity as opposed to Financial Cancer.

With a mosaic of colourful experiences available to all of us – I find it more appealing to drill deeper into life. I continually invest in a new vision or paradigm, participating in extreme adventures, that I am sure many people would find quite bizarre. A life of prosperity is a series of assignments, each one, helping you grow, developing your talents, and expanding your consciousness. As your consciousness grows, so does the impact you make and the influence within your inner circle. With this obsessive desire to acquire the ancient principles of enlightened living, I have already visited over eighty-five countries in my quest for adventure. I have dived down to the deepest abyss of the oceans, rocketed to the edge of space and summited the world's highest mountains, just to name a few.

When I was a young boy, I developed my Top 10 'Hit List' of goals to achieve in my life. I must have had quite a vision because that *hit list* is still relevant thirty years later. I strongly believe that there are no coincidences in life. A higher consciousness individual understands how prosperity laws work. A person with a compelling dream actually bends the universe to their will and strives for a unique constellation of attributes. I have three major goals remaining from my original Top 10 Hit List, which include summiting the highest mountain peak in the world, Mt Everest, visiting a space station orbiting up to 300 miles above the Earth and finally, to explore the lunar surface of the moon. This enlightened living and the manifesting of new frontiers in exploration, will serve as the next chapter in the evolution of my life.

In early adulthood, my pivotal mentor was a peak performance lecturer, author and entrepreneur by the name of Bob Proctor, who instilled in me the belief that we were all born rich. For forty years, Bob Proctor has helped create lives of prosperity, rewarding relationships, and spiritual awareness. Born in northern Ontario Canada, Bob stresses the ideas of positive thinking and self-motivation. Bob was all about 'Nik, tell me what you want and I'll show you how to get it.' Until I met Bob Proctor, I used to regard the word *rich* from a monetary perspective, but later I developed the faculty awareness to drill deeper on what he said. Bob recalled that we were all born equal, with equal opportunities and an abundance of potential. Prosperity was our natural birthright and we all possessed the same colouring marker set with which we can make our mark in life. Some of us choose black markers and white markers. Others embrace a colouring book set with a myriad of colours. Bob really had the ability to reduce the most complicated concepts in life to the simplest form.

Just recently one of my companies, Financial Freedom Institute, hosted one of the most anticipated Mind and Wealth Prosperity seminars in the US called *Wealth Celebrities*®. The *Wealth Celebrities*® event in Los Angeles, California provided a forum for the planet's most distinguished speakers to inspire, connect, contribute and stir the soul. I invited Bob Proctor as my keynote speaker and it was a privilege to share the stage and to be reunited with him again. It was also an occasion and opportunity for me to reciprocate and pay homage to his influence in my life. I was thrilled to share the exploits of my life with Bob and I sincerely thanked him. My mind had the magnetic power to attract all that I desired into my life.

The purpose of a definitive life is one that provides an oasis of enlightenment. This is the secret kindling to ignite the inner fire that lurks within us all. We all have it, some individuals make the unconscious decision to extinguish it and maintain it devoid of illumination. In life we are only measured by our contributions. It's what you give out in assisting other people to achieve their goals, once you achieved yours. Socrates said: '*The best human is all humans put together*'. I don't believe we should ever be totally satisfied with where we are in our lives. There's always the opportunity to raise our level of awareness and seize the day, *carpe diem*. By redefining our lives and seeking new vantage points, we inadvertently remove the 'IM' out of the word IM-possible. The Bannister Principle is an excellent reflection of this theory. In 1954, an Englishman, Roger Bannister ran the distance of a mile in under four minutes ... even medical experts cautioned that it was impossible to run the mile in under four minutes. Within nine months of Bannister's feat, thirty other runners achieved the milestone too. When he was asked to explain that first four-minute mile – and the art of record breaking – he answered with original directness: '*It's the ability to take more out of yourself than you've got.*' We can incorporate the Bannister Principle and implement it into the interior of our personal and business life.

One of the portraits I have on my wall in my office is a picture of a mousetrap and a mouse. What do most mice do? They come head on into the trap, flirt with the cheese and get caught. But the mouse on this portrait reminds me of the heist scene from the movie *Mission Impossible* with Tom Cruise. This particularly astute mouse on the poster has shimmied down on a vertical wire to the mousetrap to claim its cheese reward. The mouse is thinking outside the square. That's my mantra. Approach everything in life from a different angle. Unfortunately, most wandering souls approach everything in life from the same myopic angle, thus fuelling the tyranny of impoverished thinking, whereby they lose their faculty of thinking and remain captives of their negative ingrained pasts.

It is mandatory for us to cultivate our mind, hence allowing it to blossom beyond our expectations. I sincerely believe that this is the secret of happiness, where we truly find what we dearly love to do and then direct all of our energy towards doing it. Once we find out what our life's work is, we transform and undergo a sea of change and feel alive. We wake up every morning with a limitless reservoir of energy and enthusiasm for life.

My obvious enthusiasm for life has attracted lots of global attention. The television and print media of late have proclaimed me 'The Thrillionaire®'. They have classified me into a Thrillionaire® archetypal character, with my own passion points, consuming habits and creative style. With my life, I was not born into Old Money, fine art and privilege. My refinement and later sophistication of the mind was as a result of redefining my sense of purpose. I ultimately believe it is our responsibility to leave the world a better place than that we found it. It's the legacy we leave behind, the footprints we leave in history that count. We need to focus on the passions and motivations that radiate an abundance of vitality and energy in our lives, *rather than just the size of our wallets.* I am the new breed of moneyed traveller looking for high-octane adventure. Thrillionaire®s are individuals who understand the thrill of giving, and share their stories so that others will become inspired to become Thrillionaire®s themselves. Just like an inner compass guiding them towards their destination.

Look around. There is an abundance of thrills to be experienced. The quality of our thinking determines the quality of our life. We need to collect our change every day and give it to something that warms our heart. Everybody has a gift to give. If you put coins in somebody else's parking meter, send money to a child in need, sponsor endangered animals, collect change for UNICEF, give away your personal belongings to charity, lead an exhilarating heart pounding adventurous lifestyle or write a check for a massive cash donation, you are a Thrillionaire®.

The book, *The Thrillionaire®* is about my self-discovery, the exploration of my identity and mission in life. It is about wisdom I have embraced from various mentors in my life and the vision that has established my system of empowering beliefs. I created a model of the world, a map of the world that allowed me to perceive the greatest number of available choices and perspectives. *The Thrillionaire®* details my stories of adventure interspersed with financial wisdom and is purposely set out the way it is. I sincerely invite you to immerse yourself and share the powerful insights with others.

Life moves pretty fast. If you don't stop to look once in a while, you'll miss it.

THE THRILLIONAIRE® PRINCIPLE

- Once we find out what our life's work is, we transform and undergo a sea of change and feel alive. What is your life's work?
- It's the legacy we leave behind that shapes your life, what will your legacy be?
- Everybody has a gift to give, what will your gift be to the world?

Chapter 2

Journey to Titanic

If your ship doesn't come in, swim out to it – Jonathan Winters

IT ALL BEGAN WITH A NIGHT AT THE MOVIES. I had arranged to take my sister Victoria to see *Titanic*, the 1997 film about the immortalised 'unsinkable' ocean liner that struck an iceberg, sending more than 1,500 people to a watery grave. A night at the movies doesn't usually lead to the most memorable experience of a lifetime – but that night did. Something truly bizarre happened during the screening. In hindsight, I guess it was a premonition of how close I would eventually come to history's most famous shipwreck. The *Titanic* saga has captivated me ever since I was a small child.

I feel a personal connection because hundreds of passengers on board were immigrants fleeing their homeland and travelling to America, considered the new world, to pursue their dream of starting a new life.

My affinity with them is because my parents were also immigrants. My mother and father boarded ships out of Greece bound for Australia to start new lives in a continent they knew so little about. I'm sure the migrant experience isn't half as romantic as it sounds. Most immigrants have to leave their families and friends behind because they see no future in their homeland. The optimism of the migrant is an emotion that's born of despair.

On board *Titanic*, there were hundreds of people in the lowest class, steerage. When the ship went down, they were locked in, trapped, and most perished in the icy waters of the North Atlantic Ocean. There were 2,228 people on board *Titanic* when she crashed into that massive iceberg on the night of April 15th, 1912. Only 705 survived. Not only was it one of the worst maritime disasters in human history, but it was one of the most amazing. So many quirks of fate conspired to create the unthinkable. For starters, it was a moonless night. There was no reflection on the water. It was well nigh impossible for the ship's crew to see the monster lurking in the fog. *Titanic* weighed over 50,000 tonnes – she was the largest and most opulent ship in the world. She was a palace on the high seas.

The *Titanic* was the grandest ship of her time. She was majestic, lavishly decorated and considered unsinkable because four of her sixteen watertight compartments could be flooded without endangering the ship. The *Titanic* was divided into social classes according to background, wealth and education. The ship's passenger list was a cross-section of early 20th century society. On board were some of the wealthiest people in the world – a Who's Who of business and commerce types from the Old World of Europe and the New World of the Americas. And down in third class, steerage, were hundreds of desperate immigrants, all hoping that America might give them a fresh beginning. They were bound for the land of opportunity.

It was *Titanic*'s maiden voyage, which added to the pageantry and intrigue surrounding the vessel's departure from the mother country. All this drama was set against the backdrop of the new century, the last years of the industrial revolution. In a few years, the world would be at war. But, in 1912, the movers and shakers were enraptured by what engineering marvels they could build. There was a mood of optimism in the air.

James Cameron's movie of *Titanic* carried the same sense of anticipation. James Cameron is an Academy Award winning director, producer and screenwriter noted for his action/science fiction films. Cameron directed the film *Titanic*, which went on to become the top-grossing film of all time, with a worldwide gross of over US$1.8 billion dollars. He also created the *Terminator* franchise starring Arnold Schwarzenegger. *Titanic* was hailed as a blockbuster, so Victoria and I decided to see it at what we regard as the best cinema in our home city,

Melbourne. The Gold Class theatre at Crown Casino is quite exclusive and seats only twenty-five people. With a vast screen and truly captivating cinematic auditory experience, the cinema design of the Gold Class Theatre was designed to recreate the acoustics and ambience of the movie studio. So, for a three hour major epic about the most dramatic shipwreck in history, I wanted to bathe in the myriad of sensations. I certainly wasn't disappointed.

About two hours into the film, when the ship started to take on water in the movie, and the bow was filling up quickly, a freakish incident occurred. I had wanted to soak up the experience, but I hadn't expected that art would imitate life so closely. At the moment the ship was about to split in two, the cinema's sprinkler system activated. Water sprayed down from the ceiling and, within seconds, we were drenched. Talk about reality film-making! I was so caught up in the unfolding drama that it took me a few seconds to realise what was actually happening. Perhaps it was an omen. As a result of seeing that film, I seized the opportunity to get as close to the real *Titanic* as any person can. The absurdity of the drenching and the extraordinary co-incidence provoked laughter from the some of the soaked cinema fans. Others left immediately, leaving a watery trail as they filed out. People waiting in the foyer gave us weird looks as we emerged from the cinema, looking like we had just climbed out of a swimming pool in our Sunday best. Because there was no chance that the audience could resume their seats, the cinema management kindly offered us tickets to see the movie another time. I couldn't wait to get back and see the movie through.

Ever since I first read about *Titanic* in the family's encyclopedia, I had been enthralled by the story. Everything about *Titanic* was a curiosity. I remember reading how *Titanic* had four funnels, yet only three of them worked. In the day when the White Star Line commissioned construction of *Titanic*, the more funnels a ship had, the more prestigious she was considered to be. Having four funnels was a sign of grandeur, but only three of *Titanic*'s ever had steam coming out. If you see old drawings of *Titanic*, you might notice that she was often depicted with steam coming out of all four funnels. After the sinking of the *Titanic* and her sister ship *Britannic*, legend has it that shipping lines considered it unlucky to build a vessel with four funnels.

So a week after that original soaking, Victoria and I were back in the Gold Class theatre, and we watched the *Titanic* movie right through to the last frame. I didn't miss a frame of it, but I had a special reason to scrutinise the closing credits. I had been enchanted by the opening sequence, which featured modern-day images of the wreck. The pictures were so beautiful, so surreal. Here, in all her glory, was the legend. When the credits came on, I studied them to see if there was any mention of how the cinematographers had been able to film that opening sequence with the submersibles. *Titanic* lies on the floor of the North Atlantic Ocean, about 3,750 metres below the surface. To get down to that depth, and to actually film a wreck some ninety years after she sank, was an incredible achievement. As I sat through the movie, I kept thinking: If they could film the actual wreck, maybe I could go down there. So, I scanned the credits just as attentively as I had watched the film. And there it was, the following Russian entities were thanked as part of the deep sea dive – Kaliningrad-based, PP Shirshov Institute of Oceanology and the Russian Academy of Sciences. My mind started racing. In those credits was the clue that could lead me to one of the most exciting adventures of my life.

I had previously made contacts at the Yuri Gagarin Cosmonaut Space Centre in Russia during my Orbital Space Program activities in 2003, so I contacted the Shirshov Institute and was put in touch with someone who might be able to help.

After several phone calls I discovered that the MIR submersibles which were used in the deep sea dive during the making of the *Titanic* film had journeyed down to the wreck once every few years, carrying scientists, marine biologists, historians and some privileged paying enthusiasts. Paying enthusiasts? Yes! I vowed that – whatever it took – I would go down there and view the ship for myself.

In early 2005, my chance came. I was invited to undertake a dive down to the most famous sunken ship in history. Initially I was asked to complete all sorts of tests, just to ensure that I was physically and mentally suitable for the adventure. There were medical and psychological tests that I had to undertake.

They were particularly concerned about any possibility of claustrophobia, because the submersibles are just 2.1 m wide, particularly for three people spending ten hours in a pressurised biosphere at the bottom of the deepest, darkest ocean.

The management at the Shirshov Institute informed me of an expedition departing in July 2005 – and that there was only one seat left. I booked my seat. That's how I became one of the very few people in the world to ever visit the wreck of *Titanic.*

The investment in diving to the *Titanic* wreck was equal to a deposit you'd have to outlay to purchase an inner city house in my native Melbourne, Australia. For me, it was worth every cent. An adventure of this magnitude is what living is about. We were to dive down to the wreck in the month of July in the North Atlantic Ocean, as it was a month deemed to be reasonably calm and least treacherous. Other months in the Atlantic have patterns of low pressure systems that sweep across the ocean creating rogue waves. Such are the vagaries of trans-Atlantic crossings in the open sea. In the age-old battle against nature, disasters at sea have a distinctive unique appeal of human tragedy, occasional heroics and often mysterious circumstances. The *Andrea Gail*, a Gloucester Massachusetts, swordfish boat made famous in the book and movie *The Perfect Storm*, starring George Clooney and Mark Wahlberg, sank in the general vicinity of *Titanic*, just south of the tail of the Grand Banks. The Grand Banks are a group of underwater plateaus south-east of Newfoundland on the North American continental shelf. On October 28th, 1991, the *Andrea Gail* collided with monstrous storms and was left stranded in the high seas, defenceless in what meteorologists had called the 'storm of the century', when three weather systems converged in the Atlantic Ocean and created waves reported to have exceeded 100 feet.

RMS *Titanic* on her maiden voyage sank halfway between Southampton, her port of departure, and New York, the destination she never reached. At the time, she was travelling a north-westerly route and oceanographers believe she struck a *blueberg.* That's an unusually hard iceberg. It is an iceberg that has a different composition – more rocks. Against a gigantic *blueberg*, even the world's largest ship didn't stand a chance.

To meet up with the scientific research ship that would take me out to the *Titanic* wreck, I had to travel to St Johns, Newfoundland, the most remote eastern tip of Canada. The Russian research vessel *Akademik Keldysh* was in port at St Johns to rendezvous with me. This was the same Scientific Research Vessel used in the making of *Titanic* by producer James Cameron. I was also very fortunate to meet James Cameron in my July 2005 Dive, as he was filming a Discovery Channel Documentary. Cameron was using our July expedition to produce a new *Titanic* featured television event.

The Russians proudly claim the *Akademik Keldysh* to be the most lavishly fitted research ship in the world. It has several small laboratories on board, as well as a specialised library covering underwater archaeology, oceanography and deep-sea exploration. The ship has satellite communications equipment, enabling passengers to make contact with the outside world while they are in the mid-Atlantic. I'm an investor by nature, so I used the five days travelling from St Johns to the wreck site of the *Titanic* to close a couple of stock market trades. I thought I'd lock in some profit via my laptop – just in case I didn't make it back. Where there's a profit, I want to lock it in. So that's what I did. I wonder what my broker would have said about me closing trades from a research ship in the middle of the North Atlantic directly above the wreck of *Titanic*!

The *Akademik Keldysh* took the scheduled five days to get to the precise coordinates above where the wreck sits. Along the way, something unusual happened. With the extreme excitement of an expedition like this, I took along a video camera – two, in fact – and I used the camcorder to document life aboard ship. On my third day out to sea I was invited into the navigation room by the captain and everyone was quite happy for me to film the bridge. While I was looking through the viewfinder, I noticed charts on the navigator's table. A closer inspection revealed that I was inadvertently filming the exact coordinates of the *Titanic* wreck, which were marked on the map on the table. The precise location of the *Titanic* had always been a huge secret, to prevent illegal salvage operations of its treasures. I couldn't believe I was recording the precise location of history's most legendary shipwreck. I still have that footage and those coordinates.

As curious as I am, I defer to the experts of the *Akademik Keldysh* to be the caretakers of this fascinating voyage. Deep sea exploration is an extraordinarily complex process, and the men and women on board the *Keldysh* were some of the world's best. They were certainly an interesting assortment of characters. The captain and chief scientist, Dr Anatoly Sagalevitch, is a real character in particular.

At night he ushered us into his cabin for shots of vodka, and brought out his Dobro guitar, whereupon he would serenade and play Russian folk songs. Anatoly played a key role in designing the world's most advanced MIR submersibles, which can dive to depths of 6,000 metres. With Sagalevitch at the controls, the MIR submersibles were made famous in the 1997 Oscar-winning film *Titanic*.

Some of the others on board were part of James Cameron's film crew. James Cameron used our July 2005 expedition to set up the production for a Discovery Channel and IMAX documentary. On our expedition, Cameron sent down a five kilometre fibre optic cable from the Keldysh to the wreck of the *Titanic*, so that they could return a week later and record the first ever live via satellite feed from the bridge of *Titanic* for the Discovery Channel. On board the *Akademik Keldysh*, Cameron had his own production studio with millions of dollars worth of equipment.

A flamboyant passenger also on board was a Russian billionaire named Boris. Boris was an *oligarch*, one of the individuals who became so immensely rich in the privatisation of the assets of the Soviet system after its economic collapse. He obviously had a lot of clout. He and his attractive young female companion were given James Cameron's state room. It had wall-to-wall video screens and was, in itself, a mini television studio. I'd say Boris was a man of some influence. Another unique individual was Fran Capo, a close friend of mine who joined our expedition to do a book signing by the wreck of the *Titanic*. Fran has been interviewed on Good Morning America, Larry King, CNN Live among others and was featured in the Guinness Book of World Records as the fastest talking female on the planet. Fran was clocked at *603.32 words per minute*. That's ten words a second!

There were several world famous deep-sea explorers on our expedition also.

One was the highly decorated Don Walsh, who I was fortunate to interview for my *Titanic* documentary. Don was a US Navy lieutenant, who had recorded the deepest dive in history, going down to a diving depth of 35,813 feet below sea level. This dive was undertaken in the world's deepest underwater canyon, the Marianas Trench off the coast of Guam. At a maximum depth of 35,813 feet it is the deepest location on earth. He and Jacques Piccard were aboard the bathyscaphe *Trieste* when it made the record-breaking descent into the Challenger Deep. Challenger Deep is so deep that if Mt Everest were to be placed into it there would be more than two kilometres of water covering it.

Another explorer on our expedition was Ralph White who was an award-winning cinematographer who had just concluded a National Geographic documentary *Search for the Loch Ness Monster* in the Inverness Highlands in the north of Scotland. The tales of Nessie, the sea serpent-like creature that fitted a specific type of dinosaur-era sea creature called a plesiosaur has enchanted people from all over the world. Ralph White, who alongside the very famous Robert Ballard, was a key player in the expedition that discovered the wreck of the *Titanic* back in 1985. Robert Ballard also discovered the wreck of the famous World War II German battleship *Bismarck* in 1989 and had just recently discovered the famed wreck of John F. Kennedy's *PT-109* torpedo boat. In the summer of 1985, Ballard was aboard the French research ship *Le Suroît* which was using the revolutionary new side scan sonar to search for *Titanic*'s wreck. When the French ship was recalled, Ballard transferred onto a ship from Woods Hole, the *Knorr*. Unbeknownst to some, this trip was being financed by the US Navy for secret reconnaissance of the wreckage of *USS Scorpion*. The *USS Scorpion* was a top secret nuclear submarine that had sunk nearby. The agreement was that after the Navy search was concluded, Ballard would be free to hunt for *Titanic*. In 1985, Ballard came across the remains of the boilers that powered the great liner and later discovered the hull itself. *Titanic* revealed herself to the world after seventy-three years.

Whilst interviewing Ralph White for a *Titanic* documentary I was producing in 2005, Ralph informed me that he led an Anglo-French *Titanic* artifact recovery expedition aboard the EFREMER Research Vessel *Nadir* back to the *Titanic* wreck in 1987, and that he had been able to provide them the exact secret coordinates. Ralph had co-directed the salvage operation and photography during the recovery of over 1,400 artifacts from *Titanic*'s debris field, which later became the world's leading *Titanic* travelling exhibition. Ralph White recently died on February 4th, 2008. He died from complications of an aortic aneurysm at Glendale Adventist Medical Centre in California. Ralph had dived the *Titanic* wreck over thirty times and had boasted to me that he spent more time on the *Titanic* than its original captain had.

The potential for further plunder of *Titanic* has become a big issue in recent years, and – after a string of court cases – England, America and France have signed a treaty to place a moratorium on all dives down to *Titanic*. The Russians with the deepest diving submersibles in the world have yet to sign the treaty. However, there is great pressure on the Russians at the moment, and it is quite possible that expeditions such as the one I embarked on will soon be halted. While I strongly believe that wrecks should not be plundered, I obviously approve of explorers being allowed to view these surreal time capsules of the past.

It was fascinating to hear the stories of those experts aboard the *Akademik Keldysh* as it churned through the Atlantic waves towards the coordinate location above *Titanic*. I love history, particularly the stories of explorers tackling new frontiers.

As I listened to some of the worlds boldest and famed deep-sea explorers aboard the *Akademik Keldysh*, I appreciated even more just how fortunate and privileged I was.

Quite possibly, the *Titanic* will disappear in the next decade, if not because of the controversy, then most certainly because the physical wreck is being eaten away. Marine biologists are fearful that bacteria could literally chew it up within ten to fifteen years. Rusticles cling to every bit of the structure, consuming an incredible 2,000 pounds of steel every day. These microbial communities are eating away *Titanic's* iron at a rapid rate. There is precious little sea life at the bottom of the sea and, what there is, doesn't feed on bacteria. Because of the lack of ambient light at the bottom, it is pitch black. Marine biologists have taken samples of these rusticles and report that the wreck is becoming more dilapidated every year. I guess the precarious state of the wreck heightened the desire I had to go down there while I still could.

The Russian MIR Submersibles are the deepest diving vessels in the world.

The MIR submersibles can dive to a maximum depth of 6,000 metres (19,680 feet), whereas a larger submarine has only a 400 metres depth limit. The cockpit of MIR is a five centimetre thick sphere made from a combination of nickel and steel, with an inner diameter of 2.1 m. The total length of the vessel is 7.8 m and the weight 18.6 tonnes. Air pressure inside the cabin remains at a constant one atmosphere with the air being recycled in a manner similar to that used on board spacecraft. The two MIR submersibles on the *Akademik Keldysh* are part of a group of only four deep-diving vessels in the world that the Russians make available to the world's scientific community. Built of special nickel steel, they are designed to withstand the enormous pressures that exist in the depths of the oceans. The pressure on the submersible at the depth of *Titanic* is something like 6,000 pounds per square inch. The submersibles are the closest thing there is to space capsules. Travelling in them is like orbiting the planet. The compartment that accommodates three people – a pilot and two passengers – is just over two metres in diameter. Naturally, there are no bathroom facilities on board.

On August 2nd, 2007 Russia used the same MIR submersibles from my *Titanic* dive to perform the first ever manned descent to the seabed under the Geographic North Pole, to a depth of 4.3 kilometres. The historical significance of this expedition was that no human had ever travelled to the real North Pole before. The crew of MIR-1 was composed of my friend and pilot Anatoly Sagalevich and Russian polar explorer Arthur Chilingarov. On the 'real North Pole' seabed, at a depth of 4,261 metres, MIR-1 planted a one metre tall rust-proof Russian flag, made of titanium alloy and left a time capsule, containing a message for future generations. There have been historical disputes and conflicts over who reached the surface ice at 90° North first. But one could argue that, no matter who did it, the real North Pole is not a point on the ever-changing ice pack. Embracing the true spirit of adventure, its goal was a notable geographic 'first' in the exploration of our planet. The MIR descended to the unexplored Amundsen Plain, in the middle of the Arctic Ocean – the least known of all the oceans on our planet. This is a region where no human has gone before, more than 14,000 feet below the shifting polar ice cap in a dark and mysterious place.

The MIR submersibles were designed and built in Finland for the Russians during the Cold War. Their primary directives were presumably to salvage nuclear warheads from sunken Russian submarines or, alternatively, to plunder nuclear warheads from any American submarines that sank to the ocean floor. Curiously, MIR is a Russian word meaning *Peace*. Both MIR 1 and MIR 2 weigh around eighteen tonnes each. It takes a twenty-five tonne crane aboard the mother ship *Akademik Keldysh* to lift them into the water. The two submersibles dive down thirty minutes apart so that – if something goes wrong with one – the other might be able to help. At the depth of *Titanic*, I'm not sure how much help one submersible would be if another was trapped. But that doesn't worry me too much. I honestly don't concern myself with fear. My attitude is that the experience is worth any perceived risk. What's the worst scenario? That I perish down there, I suppose. Well, if I am going to exit this world in the deep blue ocean, I'd rather exit on the deck of the *Titanic*. At least, I'd be doing something that I love. Much more exciting than let's say, going out to the letter box, getting bitten by a wasp, and dying from the sting. Nah, give me *Titanic* anytime. You've probably guessed by now that I'm a curious person, and that extreme environments captivate me.

We know so little about the deep blue sea. Only three per cent of the world's oceans have ever been explored. We actually know a lot more about space than we do about our oceans. For me, shipwrecks are utterly intriguing. They are time capsules. The clock stopped the moment they sank. History has always excited me. I guess it's because of my European origins in Greece, a country so entrenched with history. It's the birthplace of civilisation and democracy. If there was a time machine, I would much prefer to go back into history than into the future. None of us can turn back time – nor can we travel through the chapters of history – but shipwrecks are perhaps the closest we come to a true time warp.

The *Titanic*, which cost a reported $7.5 million to build, is frozen in time, a time capsule of the year, 1912. That was a year when there was such optimism – the new century, the fastest and biggest ship of its time, the marvellous anticipation of its maiden voyage. *Titanic*'s crew at the time sailed faster than they should have because they wanted to get to New York one day earlier than scheduled – so they could outdo their rivals. These were the early maverick days and industrial might of the turn of the century. I have read everything I can find of the memoirs of *Titanic* survivors, the correspondence and records. Now, finally, I was close to living my dream.

We arrived at the wreck site of the *Titanic* early in the morning and began planting four transponders around the diving area. These four transponders would make it easy for the MIR submersibles to navigate within and around the wreck. On the night before my dive, at 11.40 pm, the exact time that *Titanic* struck the iceberg, I went out onto the stern of *Akademik Keldysh* and proposed my own small toast. It was a moonless night, and quite foggy. Visibility was terrible. It was just as the conditions would have been on the fateful night of April 15th, 1912. I had brought with me a Pomerol 1998 Bordeaux bottle of French red wine, and I sat there alone, and polished it off. I looked over the stern and the water was completely still – just as it was on the night of the sinking. I thought about all the unfortunate souls who had perished of hypothermia in the Atlantic's icy waters. And I remembered Frederick Fleet, up there in the crow's nest, the crewman who in 1912 first observed the impending iceberg and sounded the alarm. Alas, it was too late. The monolith of ice and stone was so close that the ship had no chance. I slept lightly that night, thinking about the lives lost, and the ghosts of that catastrophe.

Next morning, the carefully choreographed MIR support teams of the *Akademik Keldysh* hoisted our eighteen tonne submersible over the side, into the water with apparent ease. Our MIR 1 submersible pilot, Victor Nischeta, alongside myself with a fellow American passenger named Reda Anderson were the sole occupants of the biosphere. A twenty-five tonne crane using its umbilical chain attached to the submersible placed us in the water. Our capsule was lifted by a wave at this precise moment and bubbles rushed up, swirling around our porthole. The sight of entering one world and leaving another behind begins to play out in your mind. We were then towed out to sea and away from the research vessel to initiate our descent.

Victor opened up the ballast tanks, the submersible took in the sea water, and we started to dive and sink down to the murky depths of the Atlantic Ocean. Attached to no tether or chains, we were on our own. Within ten minutes, the ambient light from the portholes disappeared. All traces of sunlight were gone and we were immersed in total darkness. As we dived, we felt a surreal experience, as if we were travelling through outer space. As aquanauts, we were descending into an alien environment so potentially hostile, with close to zero chance of assistance from the outside world if we required rescuing. There was also the risk of fire in the 100 per cent oxygen internal atmosphere, hence the requirement that we wear a Nomex suit. Nonetheless, in the event of a fire at depth, it is unlikely that the Nomex suit will help us survive.

We had some guides for the early part of the journey. Victor illuminated the pitch black environment with the piercing lights of the MIR. A pod of pilot whales swam alongside our craft. They were attracted by the sonar navigation of our submersible.

The pilot whales escorted us down to about 300 metres – like caretakers of the ocean – giving us a personal tour of their domain. It was fantastic. But, as we went below 300 metres, they ditched us, as if to say: 'You guys are going far too deep.'

Reda Anderson, the other expedition member of our dive is a grandmother who lives in Beverly Hills, California. She had generated a fortune in property investment and business, and diving down to *Titanic* was one of the things she wanted to do before her time on earth had expired. It was all about doing something for the very first time for Reda. She had a contagious personality and I was invigorated by her personal triumphs. Reda also proclaimed that she was planning on becoming the oldest woman in space too. I don't doubt that at all. Several months later, Reda's life and space dream was documented in Forbes magazine. Readers were privy to absorb the chronicles of her life.

She aspired to be the oldest woman in space, and the oldest to dive so deep. At the time of our *Titanic* dive, she was seventy-six. Reda acknowledged she was taking a great risk, but she was a thrill-seeker and great company. Instead of sitting in some salon in Rodeo Drive, Beverly Hills, having her hair done or buying a new alligator purse from some designer store, Reda was all about extracting the most out of life. We talked about what motivated us, and shared the belief that life is a mosaic of experiences and chapters. She wanted to deposit as many experiences onto her mosaic before her time ran out.

Our MIR submersible was really a marvel of engineering. The acrylic plastic view ports of the submersible were about fifteen centimetres thick. Each was about twelve centimetres in diameter. They were just enough to look and film through. Mounted on the outside of the submersible was a lighting rig, which lit up everything for a distance of ten metres. I took with me two video cameras and two digital still cameras. I wasn't going to miss capturing the moment. Reda didn't bother with cameras – she just put her nose against the view port and soaked up the scenery. She absolutely loved it. The submersible also had a camera on the robotic manipular arm and an extension camera with lights. We were able to watch on a plasma screen the pictures that the outside camera was capturing.

To conserve power, the MIR submersibles run without external lights. However, Victor occasionally switched them on to allow us to observe passing marine life. The dive down into the abyss took under four hours. The sea life was unlike anything I'd ever seen. When we descended below 1,000 metres, the bio-luminescent creatures started to come into view. Bioluminescence is the production and emission of light by a living organism as the result of a chemical reaction during which chemical energy is converted to light energy. These tiny illuminated fish were something else. They virtually lit up themselves, like Christmas trees, becoming transparent. Seeing them was so exciting. 'What the hell is that?' Reda kept asking.

After three and a half hours, we finally observed it on the radar screen. My heart was rapidly pounding. It was an outline of the most awe-inspiring structure I have ever witnessed in my life. We were still twenty-eight minutes from reaching the ocean bed, yet the bow of *Titanic* was clearly visible on the radar screen. My immediate thought was that this was going to be huge. Over the next twenty-eight minutes, the image grew more vast and clearer. I could hardly wait. Exactly twenty-eight minutes had passed and then, in a moment of sheer ecstasy, we came upon the bow of *Titanic*. It was a surreal motion picture moment, simply awesome. If you remember back to childhood and how you felt when the candles lit up your birthday cake, or that first glimpse of the Christmas stocking, well, it was both of those for me.

Pressing our noses against the plastic, barely a metre from the bow, we could almost reach out and touch it. I had imagined the image so often that I had to remind myself that this was really happening. The promenade decking was still intact, so elegant, so majestic, ninety-three years after it plunged to the ocean floor. I thought of that scene from the movie, where Leonardo DiCaprio's character, Jack Dawson, balanced on the promenade decking and proclaimed he was 'King of the World'. I know it was fiction, storytelling, just a motion picture, but I'm sure people would have felt that way aboard *Titanic*. Standing on the bow of that massive liner, you would have believed you were a king or queen. My mind kept racing. I pictured the socialites of the Old World and New World swanning around on the foredeck, telling their grandiose stories of the industrial age.

The bow looked even larger than I expected. As we motored around it, up and down, I was struck by just how vast it was. And yet we were seeing only a third of the bow. The lower two thirds are embedded into the sea floor. The bow sank hard and fast, because it was filled with water. There were no air trappings in the bow. If there had been air trappings, it would have imploded the way that the stern did.

Implosions occur when air pressure outside the ship is greater than the air pressure inside.

Just above the sea bed, we came upon the anchor, covered in rusticles. I had seen the anchor in the modern-day vision in James Cameron's footage. But to see it myself, literally one metre away from it, to visit this ghost ship from the past, was as magical as being in space and orbiting around another planet.

Titanic was over 300 metres long. Every metre that we travelled, we came upon some relic, some treasure. We saw an old chest, suitcases that once belonged to immigrants, china cups, mugs, plates, wine bottles, ceramic tiles, toilets, bath-tubs, light fixtures and shoes. We saw pairs of shoes, side by side, seemingly trapped together. At that depth in the salt water, bodies and bones would have decomposed within a couple of years. Those shoes, I realised, were what remained of human bodies. The submersible had a manipulator arm which made it capable of picking up things from the ocean floor. There were so many opportunities for us to collect relics – wine bottles, tiles, shoes, even the leather suitcases that had lasted over ninety years. But we chose not to. The only souvenir I extracted from the ocean floor was a small rock from the port side of the *Titanic* bow. To me, that small rock shed light to an amazing journey and story of its own.

Thousands of small rocks are littered around the wreck of *Titanic*. They are called Ilulissat rocks because of the town of Ilulissat on Greenland's west coast. Experts believe that these rocks beside the wreck were part of the iceberg that the *Titanic* struck, and that the iceberg most likely travelled all the way from the polar ice caps of Greenland. The majority of the Icebergs in the Atlantic break away from the Ilulissat ice caps. Those rocks could have been what made the iceberg so hard. In effect, *Titanic* hit a gigantic mass of stones glued together by Ilulissat polar ice cap.

As we skimmed the ocean floor, the two MIR submersibles stayed reasonably close to each other. We were teased by the amazing sights we saw. We came across Captain Smith's cabin, with its own bath-tub. We knew where it was located from drawings of the wreck, and the contents confirmed it was indeed the captain's. We cruised past his marble bath-tub and all the copper piping, still connected. The *Titanic* was going to be Captain Smith's last voyage. The owners of the White Star Line gave him the captaincy of the greatest ship ever built as a farewell gift before he retired. Captain Smith during the final moments of the sinking apparently locked himself in the bridge with gallantry and chose to go down with his ship. As we orbited past his cabin I remembered the context of an interview he gave to a *New York Times* reporter in Southampton prior to the maiden voyage.

> I cannot imagine any condition which would cause this ship to founder. I cannot conceive of any vital disaster happening to this vessel. Modern shipbuilding has gone beyond that.
>
> *Titanic* Captain E J Smith, *New York Times* interview

Another point of interest was when we came across Molly Brown's cabin. She was the American socialite, philanthropist and activist who had come into new money.

Brilliantly portrayed in the *Titanic* movie, Molly was attempting to fit in with the fellow travellers who were of 'old money'. She had a soft side, and was very kind to the people in steerage, helping many of them onto lifeboats. She became known as 'the unsinkable Molly Brown'.

As well as exploring RMS *Titanic*, I had a scientific task to perform. The renowned deep-sea explorer David Bright, who later became a close friend, was on board the mother ship *Akademik Keldysh*. David had asked me to search and document the *Titanic*'s expansion joint section for a comparative analysis thesis he was working on. The expansion joint is the buffer in a ship's mid-section where it can stretch. This elasticity is critical for vessels to withstand impact. But with *Titanic*, significant stresses around this expansion joint soon reached the ultimate strength of the material and the giant hull fractured. David Bright told me he was using his personal dive to document photometric comparative analysis work on the *Titanic*'s structure to test if she was widening or shifting at the expansion joint. David dived the day before I did to *Titanic*, but due to time restraints and deep sea mechanical problems on his expedition, they ran out of time to closely complete his experiments.

Diving in the MIRS generally do not go according to plan as sea currents and battery failures determine the length of your mission in the deep abyss. Since I was destined for the last dive of the season, David pre-framed me where to locate the expansion joints and provided me with nautical reference maps and illustrations. When I finally surfaced many hours later after the completion of my dive, I was not 100% sure I had documented the expansion joints for David's research.

When I arrived back on board the mother ship later, David anxiously surveyed through my footage. David was so ecstatic upon realising that I did in fact have thirty seconds of expansion joint footage captured. He later told me that my footage clearly depicted the widening of the joints and validated the further deterioration of *Titanic*. After viewing my footage, David asked me for the rights to use it for his presentation talks and to showcase it to the scientific community. Months later, David informed me that the *Titanic* Historical Society in New York had an opportunity to view my expansion joint footage.

Travelling the length of *Titanic*, we moved from the bow section through the debris field until we eventually came to the stern. It's quite hard to work out which pieces belong to the stern. It looks like the entire stern had gone through a food processor.

The chaos actually surprised me. It's obvious the stern imploded on impact. When *Titanic* hit the iceberg, the ship buckled, and thousands of rivets came undone. The impact was on the starboard side. Resting on the ocean floor, the bow and stern lie about 600 metres apart, facing in opposite directions. The stern must have twisted on the way down and imploded. There are thousands of items shattered all over the place. The disappearance of the crow's nest is another indicator of how the steel structure is rapidly deteriorating. The crow's nest was observed and recorded during a 1998 dive. But it has since broken off and fallen away. That's a measure of the rapid rate of decay. Now all that remains of the crow's nest is a hole in the mast that lies over the forecastle. We cruised above the mast and peered into the hole where the crow's nest was. It was there that Frederick Fleet cried out, 'Iceberg right ahead, iceberg!'

Cruising around the wreck for several hours, we discovered the ocean floor littered with debris from the wreck. At the stern section, when we were viewing the propellers, we had a very close call. In order to get down to the propellers, we went deep into the aft section of the stern, beneath the overhanging promenade decking which – at any time – could have entombed us. No-one mentioned the risk. A piece of promenade decking dropped on our MIR, smashing into pieces because of its decayed state. We were forced to use the manipulator arm to wrestle off the remaining piece of promenade decking. I have this magical moment captured on video. I dare say that if a submersible got entangled or if a larger piece of debris happened to fall on us, the situation would not have been pleasant. Still, we didn't discuss potential negatives. Reda was fearless. Like me, all she wanted to do was to get as close as possible to *Titanic* and its giant propellers.

We took with us a packed lunch, and Victor had a treat in mind for us. He piloted the submersible cautiously onto the ship's bridge and parked it. We sat there for a half hour and ate lunch. What an eerie feeling and environment. This was the exact same location where Captain Smith had once stood as the doomed liner capitulated to the sea. What a surreal episode I was experiencing. I was literally one metre from the steering gear telemotor section of the bridge which Captain Smith once clutched in his grip. Was it a safe parking spot? Well, we had parked an eighteen tonne MIR submersible vessel on a sheet of two centimetre thick steel that had been eroding and rusting away for ninety-three years. You decide. Ah well, lunch was good. We had packed a few sandwiches, a couple of chocolate bars and an orange juice. Upon my return to Australia I was informed by certain media groups that I officially became one of the first in the world to dine on the deck of the *Titanic* since the actual sinking in 1912. An eerie ghostlike feeling enveloped my thoughts.

After a late lunch, Victor blew the ballast tanks using compressed air, and the MIR became positively buoyant again, allowing us to rise to the surface. Victor was quite relaxed about everything. So calm in fact that he and Reda both seemed to nod off to sleep during parts of the slow journey ascent to the mother ship. Reda was exhausted. I was wide awake, kicking back and listening to music on my ipod. I sat there thinking about all the marvellous sights I had just witnessed, and staring at the luminescent fish, flicking the lights on myself.

It took me several days to come down from that high. I enjoyed the celebratory glass of champagne back on board the *Akademik Keldysh* with Anatoly, Victor and Reda but I didn't need it. I was stimulated enough. That experience was contagious for me. Before going down to *Titanic*, I had known very little about the other great shipwrecks of the world. On board the *Akademik Keldysh*, however, I heard about less famous liners that had sunk, and our famed team of deep sea divers aboard the Keldysh spoke of the doomed fate that befell *Titanic*'s sister ships, *Britannic* and Olympic. *Titanic* is immortalised. It's like Neil Armstrong. Everyone knows the first man to walk on the moon. But who remembers the most recent person to walk on the moon? His name is Eugene Cernan and he strolled on the lunar landscape during Apollo 17, the last Apollo mission, the last human to walk the surface of the moon in 1972.

Aboard the Keldysh, I heard a lot about *Britannic*, the sister ship of the *Titanic*, from my friend and renowned adventurer David Bright. A few years ago David headed a team of US Navy divers that salvaged the USS *Monitor*, which was the first ironclad warship commissioned by the United States Navy and used in the American civil war. Upon her salvage from her murky depths, David and the other divers discovered the remains of two trapped crew members from 1863, who were later given full military funerals.

Tragically, my good friend David Bright died in a deep sea diving accident in August 2006, a year after our *Titanic* dive. He had the most recorded dives down to the *Andrea Doria*, the fabled Italian super line that sank off Nantucket in 1956 after it struck a Swedish liner called the Stockholm. David was on a new record dive of the *Andrea Doria* when he died. After a long, deep dive, a diver is required to carry out decompression stops to avoid the bends. The bends or decompression illness as it is medically known is generally caused when a diver surfaces too rapidly from depth. Air contains eighty per cent nitrogen, which at the surface is inhaled and exhaled without effect. At pressure this nitrogen is forced into the bloodstream and if a diver ascends from depth without allowing sufficient time to 'off-gas', nitrogen bubbles can form, leading to the bends. In David's case, during his ascent, he decompressed too fast and suffered a massive stroke. I know it's a cliché when it's said that someone died doing what they loved, but David truly loved deep sea diving. He was a gentle giant and amazing person. He was an inspiring character to be around. When you've done things so many times, I guess you can become a little complacent.

On our voyage to *Titanic* in 2005, we spoke for many hours about mounting an expedition to explore the wreck of the *Britannic*, *Titanic*'s sister ship, which lies at a depth of 500 feet, off the island of Kea, sixty-four kilometres south-east of Athens, Greece. With my command of the Greek language and networking contacts in Greece we could document the *Britannic* and produce a documentary for the Discovery or National Geographic Channel in the US. We had planned our expedition to the watery grave of the *Britannic* for June 2007, but due to David's death, I postponed all dive plans. I still intend to go ahead with the *Britannic* expedition and will mount an expedition at a later date in honour of David.

So far, there have only been three major expeditions down to *Britannic*. The first was the 1976 discovery of the wreck by a team led by legendary explorer Jacques Cousteau. The second was in 1998, and the only other was in 2003. The reason why there have been so few dives is that it isn't easy to get permission from Simon Mills, the Englishman who now owns the *Britannic* wreck, and also the protective Greek Government who discourages diving to the wreck. I have made contact with Simon, and he would support an expedition to the wreck. We both share and respect an appreciation for the *Britannic*, and the role she played in the saga of the ill-fated vessels of the White Star Line. *Britannic* was built in the same shipyard as *Titanic*. She was the new unsinkable ship – over thirty metres longer than *Titanic*. But, when World War One broke out, the opulent cruise liner was re-commissioned and taken over by the Admiralty as a Red Cross hospital ship. She was never to sail as the luxury liner that her owners had in mind.

She sailed off to war with 625 crew and 500 doctors, nurses and Royal Army Medical Corps personnel aboard. On November 21st, 1916, as she pushed through the Kea Channel off Athens, heading to Salonica to pick up wounded Allied troops from the ill-fated Gallipoli campaign, she was struck, either by a German mine or U-boat.

She sank in just fifty-five minutes – three times faster than *Titanic*. *Britannic* became the largest cruise liner ever sunk. The most sensational feature of the wreck of the *Britannic* is that it is still in one piece, resting on her starboard side. Even the fabled Marconi radio room is still intact. Twenty-one people died. They were killed when lifeboats were drawn into the whirling propellers.

The remaining survivors were picked up by naval patrol vessels. The third sister of the White Star Line, Olympic, was also doomed. She had a dismal record for collisions and ended up as a spare parts ship.

Mounting an expedition to *Britannic* will not be an easy dive. The strong current and the vagaries of ocean diving make it a very challenging project. But I want to document the *Britannic* and to thoroughly explore this extraordinary time capsule. During the most recent expedition, divers discovered such treasurers as the metal frame of the chandelier that hung above the grand staircase. Even china items with the White Star logo were found. I want to discover what is left of the fabled Marconi room, the Turkish baths and other features that are part of folklore. *Britannic* is so integral to the *Titanic* saga. Having witnessed the awesome beauty of *Titanic*, now it's my dream to explore her sister ship and fulfil a promise I made to my good friend, David Bright.

THE THRILLIONAIRE® PRINCIPLE

- How much have you extracted out of life?
- Life is a mosaic of experiences and chapters, what are yours?
- How many experiences have you deposited onto your mosaic?

Chapter 3

Life origins

Wanting something is not enough. You must hunger for it. Your motivation must be absolutely compelling in order to overcome the obstacles that will invariably come your way – Les Brown

When I was eight, a travelling salesman knocked on the front door of our house in Port Melbourne and sold my non-English speaking parents a set of the Encyclopaedia Britannica. The salesman probably laughed all the way to the bank. He must have known that my father, a truck driver, and mother, a machinist at a car factory, could ill-afford such an expensive outlay. But the salesman's spiel was good. He probably thought his pitch was flawless. He advised my parents how the thick volumes with their plush leather lining would assist the kids with their homework and offer advanced learning.

I was the youngest of four siblings, and we were all standing in the background, nodding impatiently. I remember yelling out, 'Let's get them, let's get them!'

Our parents always put our education first, so they signed up to buy the set of Encyclopaedia Britannica – even though the purchase was probably beyond their means. That set of encyclopaedia turned out to be one of the greatest influences on my life.

It was the spark that set my imagination on fire. The gateway to knowledge was unleashed. In the 1970s if you walked into a home and the Encyclopaedia Britannica was on the bookshelf, you immediately knew that you were in a home where higher learning and discovery were respected and cherished.

The discoveries I made through reading the Encyclopaedia Britannica as a young child were simply breathtaking. They opened me up to the dreams that I would fulfil in adult life. I would read the encyclopaedia in family time and – without my parents knowing – I'd take them to bed with me, too. But bedtime for me meant grabbing an encyclopaedia and sneaking it into my bedroom so I could read in the dark. I'd shine a torch under the sheets, flick the pages of a volume through to a subject that fascinated me, and I'd read until I nodded off to sleep. The volume containing the *Space* chapter got a real workout from me. *Space* was indeed my true fascination. The pages of that chapter were so well-thumbed and dog-eared. I could never get enough of travelling into other dimensions. Sometimes I'd stay awake past midnight, dreaming about the things I was going to pursue in life, and imagining the world that was out there waiting for me.

All that reading had its down side, though. My eyes suffered badly. My parents made an appointment for me to see an optometrist who recommended I wear glasses for my short-sightedness – but I disliked the glasses chosen for me, and refused to wear them. I'll tell you about the resolution to that problem later in this chapter. My eyesight at the time was abysmal, but my vision for the future did not diminish. The encyclopaedia opened up to me all the things I wanted to accomplish. From the age of four through until I was eleven, I wanted to be an astronaut. That was my main goal. It was every boy's dream to become an astronaut and travel to space, but I really believed and lived the dream of it. Those volumes exposed me to a mosaic of experiences, a whole kaleidoscope of flavours that I wanted to taste, feel and explore.

These days the Encyclopaedia Britannica is available on CD-ROM, but nothing will ever replace those rich, thick, bound volumes. It's a different feeling of absorption when you touch the page. There's escapism in those volumes and for me, they were magic. My mother still has that very same set of Encyclopaedia Britannica in her home today. That very same set that so inspired me a long time ago.

It was then that I pretty much laid down the framework for my goals and dreams. I sat down and wrote out all the things I wanted to accomplish.

Without knowing it, at the age of eight I wrote the screenplay of my life. Mapping out my objectives and my goals released the creative juices which set me on my path of purpose. To live life to the fullest, you must stand guard at the gate of your garden to allow the pinnacle of all information to enter. By choosing my thoughts I constructed the picture of prosperity in order for it to be manifested. The great artist Vincent Van Gogh was asked how he painted such beautiful work. Van Gogh said, 'I dream my painting, and then I paint my dream.' In other words, he vividly illustrated the picture in his mind first and then he made a replica on canvas-in oil, of the original visualisation in his mind. In truth, there has never been an *original* 'Van Gogh' sold!

Another inspirational character for me in childhood was a comic book adventurer named Tintin. The *Adventures of Tintin* (French: *Les Aventures de Tintin*) is a series of Belgian comic books created by Belgian artist Hergé. Tintin, a young Belgian reporter and traveller, who was aided by a colourful cast of characters. Tintin books remain both unrivalled in their complexity and depth even after more than a half century. There is an infinite variety of themes coupled with a select squadron of quirky characters. To date two hundred million copies of this globetrotting boy journalist's adventures have been sold worldwide and the books have been translated in over fifty languages.

Tintin was living the 'never grow up' dream and I travelled the world through his pages, taking in every exotic detail. I came across the Tintin books, which were written in the 1930s and 1940s, on the shelves of the library at my primary school. Every lunch-time I headed straight for the library to read Tintin. Our school library had the entire series of about twenty-three books, which I read and re-read, daydreaming about the magical world that Tintin inhabited. In his various adventures he was a pilot, space explorer, mountain climber and deep-sea diver. He also climbed the mountains of Nepal, rescued African slaves, battled pirates and dived down to the deepest abyss of the ocean to explore shipwrecks.

When not adventuring in some exotic location, our seemingly permanent adolescent hero, Tintin, lived with his amiable but accident-prone friend, Captain Haddock. Captain Haddock lived the good life in a huge country mansion, Marlinspike Hall, on a very expensive estate. He had his own butler,

Nestor, and was surrounded by an assortment of memorabilia from his exploits with Tintin. I deduced that – lacking a wealthy friend such as Captain Haddock, if I wanted to become an adventurer like Tintin – I too would need to develop multiple pillars of income in order to afford such a lifestyle. When I reflect back on the adventures of Tintin, I realised that the actual adventures I had personally embarked on thus far in my life, had been remarkably similar to his. On my travels through life I've lost count of the times that I've been in some far-flung destination and had this weird feeling of *deja-vu,* suddenly realising that I was having a Tintin flashback.

Snowy, an exceptionally white wire fox terrier, is Tintin's four-legged faithful companion who travels everywhere with him. The bond between the dog and Tintin is deeper than life, and they have saved each other from perilous situations many times.

Years later, I adopted a small sidekick dog of my own by the name of Cassiopeia who had been abandoned by her previous owners. I had managed to save her life from certain euthanasia at the RSPCA, The Royal Society for Prevention of Cruelty to Animals. After adopting her as my own, I reflected upon the everlasting spirit and influence of Tintin and Hergé that would later serve me in adulthood. Alongside other Tintinologists, my childhood remained in a blissful trance. Tintin addicts would also be pleased to hear that Steven Spielberg and Peter Jackson, the director of *The Lord of the Rings* have announced a three-part trilogy and picture deal to finally bring Tintin to the big screen. Tintin is also currently enjoying a renaissance with a London stage show.

Growing up, I suffered a host of setbacks through childhood. Life in the real world rarely goes to plan. Fatigue and illness has the potential to dominate the lives of those who are living without direction and dreams. When I was barely a month old, my parents were advised by hospital staff that had I developed chronic asthma. My mother later told me that things were 'touch and go' for some time. The supposed asthma diagnosis and the later short-sightedness episode of my life conspired to derail my boyhood dreams. In school, I could barely see the blackboard and used to sit near the front of the class so I could read what the teacher was writing on the board.

Reality bites. When I was eleven my father gave me a stern appraisal of how poorly my life was going. He told me in no uncertain terms that I should stop wasting my time dreaming about becoming an astronaut. 'You have asthma, you are short-sighted, and you are failing mathematics,' he told me. 'These are three reasons why you will never, ever become an astronaut'. I was shattered. My mind had lost its lustre, and perhaps my most human endowment, my spirit. Things could not have been any worse. Of course, he was right. I was poor at maths, short-sighted and now had become a stressed-out boy who was labelled as an asthmatic. Stress causes your precious mental energy and spirit to leak, just like the inner tube of a tyre.

My father was a hard-working truck driver. He carted gravel for a cement company around the state of Victoria in Australia. He always left for work so early that I never saw him in the morning, and he usually got home from work after we had gone to bed. At times he was gone for over a week. He worked long hours to ensure his children had food on the table and a private schooling education.

His name was Konstantinos Halikopoulos (which was later cut short to Halik in the mid-1970s). My parents chose to shorten our surname because almost everyone misspelt or mispronounced it. I was born Nikos Halikopoulos. Both my parents had emigrated from the Peloponnese region, a large peninsula in southern Greece. The Peloponnese owes its name to the mythological hero Pelops, a legendary king of the city of Mycenae. In historical times, the Peloponnese was mostly populated by Dorians under the leadership of the ruling Spartans from Sparta.

My father was a complex character, an enigma. He was born in the historical village of Hora, Messinia. Hora was built on a hilltop and has preserved its old-fashioned appearance – stone houses with tiled roofs and narrow lanes. Just outside my father's village of Hora lies the famous ruined palace of Nestor, who took part in the Trojan War. Nestor was an Argonaut, who was part of a band of heroes who, in the years before the Trojan War, accompanied Jason and the other Argonauts in his quest to find the Golden Fleece.

The 1930s in Greece was the period of the Great Depression. My father was the youngest of nine children and whose five older siblings died of disease and malnutrition. His parents were so poor that they gave him away to the Fotopoulos couple of Gargaliani who were wealthy land owners but couldn't have children. Gargaliani sits on a lush hillside with a magical carpet of olive trees and vines that stretch out to the sea. My father was only two-years-old when he was adopted by the Fotopoulos couple and was never reunited with his real parents until the age of eighteen. He met his biological parents for a brief time and forever remained angered at their decision to give him away. My father's biological parents begged him to forgive them. In the subsequent years of that visit, my father lived the life of a nomad until he joined the Greek Army as a soldier at twenty-two years of age.

He grew up hard, and music was his only friend. As a teenager, he learnt to play a famous Greek stringed instrument called a bouzouki and performed in the main Greek taverns of Hora, Gargaliani and Athens. In his late twenties he moved to Athens, like so many Greeks, hoping that the big city might provide opportunity. He continued to perform professionally as a bouzouki player in late night taverns. When he told me about those days, he would shake his head and say that musicians were at the bottom of the barrel in Greek society. He talked of the seedy bars, the womanising, the drinking and the lowlife. He never wanted his children to become musicians.

Greece in the 1950s was riddled with poverty. Unemployment was high. My father wanted to emigrate to America or Canada, but the only immigration option given to him was Australia. The island continent in the South Pacific needed as much labour as it could get. He had never heard of Australia until the week before his ship left the port of Piraeus, bound for Melbourne. He longed for a new life, a chance to start afresh, and he took what he was given. The voyage to Australia took three months.

Konstantinos Halikopoulos arrived in Melbourne on July 7th, 1959, three years after that city hosted the Olympic Games. His possessions consisted of an old leather suitcase, enough clothes for a few days, his bouzouki and a little red book that he carried everywhere. My father would never hear or see from his real parents or the Fotopoulos couple ever again.

My father had endured a lot of tough times and had formed some strong opinions, based on his working class ideologies. He was a proud socialist. The little red book he brought with him on the ship was the communist manifesto of Chairman Mao Tse-tung. He carried a Greek translation version of Mao's doctrine. There was a hammer and sickle on the front cover, and he carried it around everywhere. He was vehemently anti-capitalism, anti-western society. Fidel Castro and Ho Chi Minh were among his peers that he respected. He carried that little red book for decades and I can tell you the exact day that he finally discarded it. It was the day that the Berlin Wall came down in 1989 and the unravelling of the Iron Communist Curtain was finally a reality. He threw it in a pit of fire in front of me. There and then, he finally accepted that the utopian ideology of socialism had proven itself to be a failed political experiment. He was devastated by the sight of the food queues in communist countries, the long lines of people just waiting to get bread. He had believed that communism would deliver equality for all people, a balance of equilibrium and prosperous societies.

My mother Dionisia Antonopoulos had left her remote village of Raftopoulo in the upper mountain regions of the Peloponnese, in southern Greece. If the economic circumstances in Athens were dire, they were appalling in the mountain village of Raftopoulo. Many young people fled the hills in the hope of finding work in Athens. My uncle Nick Antonopoulos had arrived in Australia before my mother and promised his sister that upon finding work, he would send for her. My mother didn't hesitate to leave Greece when he finally sent her the money for passage to Australia in 1958. She wanted to take the chance – even if it meant travelling alone. In 1959 my parents were introduced to one another and within one month they were married. Their first home, ironically enough, was located less than a mile from where their immigrant ships had come ashore at Station Pier in Melbourne for the first time.

My father's beliefs were contrary to my mother's, who was a devout Orthodox Christian. Before she came to Australia, she had never travelled outside her village in Greece. She remembers, upon boarding the ship for the very first time, seeing her first black person. Until that moment, she had no comprehension that black people existed. It was 1958 when she set sail. My mother left behind her old life, but she kept her values. Despite my father's alternative religious beliefs, she remained a strict Orthodox Christian. They agreed to send their children to catholic schools, because my father had at least conceded that Catholic schools would provide a sound education.

My parents always considered our education to be the top priority in their lives.

They wanted to give us what they had been denied – scope to plan for the future.

We all attended private schools – I had my primary schooling at Resurrection Primary School in the suburb of Essendon and secondary schooling at Catholic Regional College in St Albans and Sydenham.

By the time we advanced to secondary school, we were living in the working class suburb of Airport West, near Melbourne's international and domestic airports. My parents worked slavishly to put us through private school. Seventy per cent of household income was allocated to pay the school fees. My father even nominated the professions that he wanted each of us to pursue. He decided that the oldest child, Dimitrios (Jim) would become a doctor. The second oldest, Georgia, would become a criminal lawyer and Victoria would study psychology to graduate as a psychologist. My father had plans for me to pursue law also. In his opinion, law, psychology and medicine were the only prosperous and honourable fields we could enter into. Jim would indeed study medicine, Georgia did graduate as a criminal lawyer and Victoria majored in behavioural psychology. As for me, I permanently deferred from university all together. My path lay elsewhere. A well-worn path wasn't necessarily the right path for me to follow.

While my father was a hard-worker and had a strong philosophy, in hindsight I believe he did lack some skill in parenting. Looking back, it must have been a strange household – we had an atheistic socialist father and a devout, orthodox Christian mother with four kids being privately educated in the Catholic schooling system. My mother's house was a shrine, paying homage to the Lord. My father's philosophy was that he felt religion was a divider of people, a phoney, and that it pandered to weak people. His belief was that people should create their own happiness, and not rely on the activities of praying and wishing. He would comment that religion makes you wish that someone will save you, that people pray to be taken care of. Like my father, I believe power is in our own hands. We create our own destiny and fortunes in life. He would often complain that there were more churches in the world than shelters to assist the poor in need of food. I agreed with him on that. I embraced the theories from him about claiming ownership of my life. From an early age, I thought independently. I knew I had to create my own disciplines for my own goals.

I grew up influenced by his anti-religious philosophies and my mother's diet of forced religion. Through this combined parental influence, I developed an agnostic view in regards to religion early on. Growing up, I was looking for one belief system to cling onto but then I realised you don't have to, so long as you find something that gives you peace. But like my father, I am adamant that the most qualified person in the world will always be ourselves. The moment we rely on any external force, entity or factor, we automatically, in effect by law, become disempowered.

My siblings and I were all well educated. We share common goals. We're all about giving back and contributing to society as much as we can. Our parents wanted to provide as much opportunity as they could for us. They wanted us to achieve excellent grades and find prosperous jobs. My parents wanted society to be proud of us. That meant they worked from first light until dark every day. My parents continued to work laboriously, even after they acquired their first three properties. Because my parents went to work before I woke in the morning, my sisters Georgia and Victoria took care of me. They would wake me, make sure I showered, and provide food for me on the breakfast table. My parent's health deteriorated rapidly as a result of their hard work. My father suffered crippling back injuries for most of his life and my mother developed severe varicose veins throughout her life.

My personal health became an issue too – by the age of eleven, my eyesight was so poor that I couldn't see what the teachers were writing on the blackboard. I was receiving poor grades. The eye specialist put it down to my continual reading in bed. I used to go to bed every night with the Encyclopaedia Britannica or

Hergé's Tintin books. The specialist prescribed me glasses, but I refused to wear them. I viewed the wearing of glasses as a disability. I didn't want to be reliant on anything. I would do anything I could to avoid having to rely on glasses.

Playing guitar was soon to become a major influence in my life. One rainy afternoon in 1979, my brother Jim and I were watching a television documentary about Jimi Hendrix. I thought Hendrix was really cool. He was incredibly innovative and unlike any other guitarist the world had heard. Hendrix was considered to be one of the greatest and most influential guitarists in rock music history.

I had formative guitar lessons in the early days and rapidly progressed. By the age of twelve, I had surpassed the talents of my first guitar tutor who was allocated the task of teaching me. A spark of life had begun to flicker and the most golden opportunity to rekindle the passionate inner fire in me soon developed. After the extinguishing of my astronaut dreams, music would later consume my life. By thirteen, I was practising guitar for three hours after school. I dedicated my life to music. Even at thirteen, I started teaching guitar to people twice my age. I advertised my guitar lessons on the notice boards of music shops. Students used to come to the door of my family home and ask for guitar lessons and, when I answered, they would ask: 'Is Nik Halik here?' When I said I was Nik, they'd laugh. I was half their age and size, who can blame them for laughing. If they needed convincing, I'd challenge them to give me a chance and play a few tunes to show them what I was capable of.

From the age of fourteen, I grew my hair longer – so I could emulate Jimi Hendrix.

Soon I knew more about playing guitar than my second tutor. My development as a guitarist was relentless. I've always been the sort of person who, when I take something on, I get proficient at a very fast rate. I progressed through several tutors by the age of seventeen. Soon, I virtually ran out of tutors in my home town of Melbourne to be inspired by. I had an entire catalogue of students, of which some were professional performing musicians. I was charging up to $25 an hour, a tidy sum of money for a teenage boy, and it was giving me the capital to upgrade my ownership of more expensive guitars and amplification equipment.

By the age of seventeen, I had also saved $30,000. I used this money to fund my first big move – I started making plans to re-locate to Los Angeles in the US to study guitar with the best teachers on the planet. At age seventeen, I permanently deferred from university. My dream was to become a great guitarist and performing musician. As you'd expect, the notion of this disgusted my father, but my dearest and caring mother supported me. She told my father that they had placed great expectations on the three older children, but that they should allow the youngest one to follow his dreams. 'He'll find his way,' she said. It must have been hard for my father to accept, particularly as I wanted to move and live in the US, the land of Uncle Sam, the birth of capitalism and the dollar bill.

My father had been my musical influence because of his bouzouki playing, but he never wanted his children to become musicians. He didn't want me to travel the same path as he did – the seedy bars, the nightlife, getting home at 5 or 6 o'clock in the morning. He was about earning respect by having an honest job. He did, however possess perfect musical pitch, a perfectly tuned ear for music. His children inherited that gift. Even as a young boy, I was able to hear a piece of music and within minutes, I could transcribe the work for my students. I still have that uncanny naturally born gift. A jet can fly past, and I could tell you the musical pitch of it.

I recall my students would come to lessons, hand me a cassette tape of a song, such as Deep Purple's *Smoke on the Water* or Led Zeppelin's *Stairway to Heaven* or The Eagles' *Hotel California* and I would transcribe the music and guitar solo for them.

In those days, very few people could transcribe these works, which in effect validated me to charge an additional monetary premium.

What spurred me to go to the US was that I earned myself a scholarship entry to the famous Guitar Institute of Technology (GIT), the world's most innovative school of contemporary music. The Guitar Institute of Technology was part of the Musicians Institute in Hollywood, California. It offered a comprehensive, hands-on education in contemporary music performance.

GIT was the equivalent to studying law at Harvard University or studying science and technology at MIT in Cambridge, Massachusetts. I had seen an advertisement for the GIT in *Guitar Player* magazine, and knew that my musical destiny involved studying there and moving to Hollywood. I moved to Hollywood, California in my late teens, to study at GIT. It was an awe inspiring arsenal of the world's greatest musicians. The institute was open 24/7 with over 300 of the world's upcoming musical students in attendance.

I vividly remember my first week in Hollywood. An earthquake along the San Andreas Fault measuring a magnitude of 5.0 on the Richter scale struck the greater city of Pasadena and Downtown LA. I also witnessed the carnage of two bullet-ridden limousines whilst travelling east along San Bernardino Freeway Interstate 10. Welcome to LA.

Hollywood, situated west-north-west of downtown LA, was the cultural identity and historical centre of the major movie studios. When I arrived there in 1988, an abundance of prostitutes, panhandlers, drug dealers and the homeless swelled her ranks. Hollywood had fallen into many years of serious decline. Tourists who came to Hollywood in order to view where the stars dined, played, shopped or lived were disappointed to witness the polar opposite.

I used to walk along Hollywood Boulevard from the apartment I was renting on the way to GIT and along the way I would brush past all the scientology spruikers, drug dealers, prostitutes and pimps hawking their wares. The stars were there alright – on the pavement only, the Hollywood walk of fame featuring the likes of Marilyn Monroe, John Wayne, Elizabeth Taylor and others. Hollywood, since 2001, is at last now undergoing rapid gentrification and revitalisation.

My decision to leave Australia was all about being inspired, to feel more alive and to fuel unbridled energy into my life. My natural curiosity to being mentored by the world's elite musicians was to provide the creative spark I needed. Within a fortnight of arriving in LA, I joined my first US band. We would often jam until 4 am. The band was headed by Derek, a half Cherokee Indian and myself on lead guitar. Both Derek and I were 'shredders', which is someone who 'cuts heads with the devil'. It was great stuff – a throwback to the 1930s, when the blues artists would travel to the Mississippi crossroads to sign a deal with the devil in return for fame, going head-to-head against each other. We were forever attempting to outperform and challenge each other to greater heights. Performing is an amazing experience. It's the feeling of entertaining, rather than being entertained. You're sharing a melodic story with an audience. There is no feeling more powerful that having an audience that is dialling into your zone. Being a musician on stage, it's like you're having sex with the audience. Of course, groupies came with the territory. I had no idea that so many women would be attracted to vocalists and lead guitarists in particular.

Any former musician will tell you that they miss the lifestyle of being on the road and touring. But a savvy and mature musician will also preach that you take heed of their advice to aerate your mindset or quite possibly, to disassociate yourself from the industry and save your soul. I spent over three years in LA and lived the rock guitarist lifestyle. It was a blast. Living and experiencing the culture of LA was my personal odyssey of self discovery. I returned home to Australia years later, 300 per cent matured.

THE THRILLIONAIRE® PRINCIPLE

- Have you experienced a spark of life which had begun to flicker?
- Life in the real world rarely goes to plan, are you enjoying the greatness of the moment?
- Fatigue and illness has the potential to dominate the lives of those who are living without direction and dreams, does your life currently have direction?

Chapter 4

A new window onto the world

Every great achievement was once considered impossible – Anonymous

At the Buena Vista Street exit on the 134 Westbound, came the most remarkable news of my life. A radio advertisement about a revolutionary eye surgery from the Soviet Union had reached the shores of America. The Soviet Union were medical innovators with the most revolutionary surgical procedures. Naturally these innovations were not available to the West. The Soviet Union was crumbling and the protest movement, dubbed 'Perestroika', was gaining strength in the late eighties. The might of her power and her iron curtain grip on Eastern Europe were disintegrating. This meant Soviet medical pioneers were looking to the United States to commercialise their medical discoveries. My eyes for the first time in a decade seemed bright, offering a window into this extraordinary vitality of news. I quickly veered off and pulled to the side of the road in search of a pen to write down the name and number advertised. Unable to find a pen, I even attempted to engrave it on some paper with my thumbnail. Fortunately, I was able to memorise both the number and name of the man responsible for providing this opportunity of a lifetime to me. It was a gentleman by the name of Ronald P Jensen.

He was advocating a new eye surgery for the cure of short-sightedness. In haste, I made contact with his clinic in Glendale, on the eastern end of the San Fernando Valley and met him. Ronald P Jensen told me, 'Nik you need to know and understand the side effects, this surgery is revolutionary and in some ways, it's still experimental, do you still wish to proceed?' Jensen explained that the procedure was called 'radial keratotomy'. Radial keratotomy was the first surgical procedure to be widely used to correct nearsightedness and was invented by the eminent Soviet eye surgeon Svyatoslav Fyodorov in the Soviet Union in 1973. In radial keratotomy, microscopic incisions are made on the surface of the cornea in a radial, or spoke-like, pattern. The effect is that the light rays entering the eye, which have been focused in front of the retina, focus closer to the retina instead, resulting in clearer vision.

Fyodorov's story is the stuff of medical legend. An iron-ore miner who wore glasses had steel shrapnel accidentally lodged in the cornea of his eyes. Fyodorov treated the miner and extracted all debris from his eyes. The miner weeks later declared to Fyodorv that he no longer required the use of his optical glasses and claimed his vision had vastly improved after the shrapnel was removed from his cornea. Fyodorov, asked himself, if accidental cuts can improve vision, what could precision cuts do? Practising at first on rabbits, he deduced the correct number and length of cuts needed to reshape the cornea and deliver twenty-twenty vision. He also designed a special diamond blade critical to the procedure.

Fyodorov had set up clinics in Soviet-friendly countries, running them like medical factories. It was like a conveyor belt where patients would lie down on the bed, and it would slide through a stainless steel door and the patient would stop at the first surgeon under a microscope. Each surgeon performed a specific task, and then the conveyor belt brought around the next patient. A chief surgeon, occasionally Fyodorov, supervised from a video control room.

As I agreed to undertake this revolutionary operation, Ronald P Jensen provided me with a contract to sign, which I did. It briefly read as follows: 'Radial keratotomy carries risks, sometimes causing problems with night vision and glare. It is also liable to complications that may lead to severe visual impairment, blindness, or loss of an eye.'

Yes, your eyes, and these are the only ones you're going to get for the rest of your life. What was I thinking? The operating day was scheduled. I telephoned my parents and advised them of the impending operation and that there was absolutely nothing to worry about. When I mentioned the Soviet connection, my father was impressed.

Ronald P Jensen heard about Dr Fyodorov's breakthrough, so he flew the Russian to Los Angeles to teach him. Back then, in 1988, the surgery cost about US$7,500 which was roughly equal to the deposit on a house.

The surgery was staggered. He operated on one eye one week and the other a week later. That sounded reassuring to me. At least if I went blind as a result of the surgery in one eye, I had a week to pull out and save the other eye. Crazy, I know.

The surgery in Ronald P Jensen's clinic took just twenty minutes on each eye. Jensen operated under local anaesthetic. When both eyes were eventually operated on, it was an amazing relief. Everything was so bright – the sky, trees, buildings. Suddenly, things became more definite. I realised then just how badly my eyes had deteriorated. The world was up close and in focus. A continuous spectrum of luminous light and the rainbow of colours came into view. The golden keys to radiant health, my lasting happiness and inner fulfilment were indeed a reality. It was a great day to be alive.

Ronald P Jensen's prior Australian patients for the radial keratotomy procedure included two Qantas pilots who required their vision to be corrected to twenty-twenty in order to continue flying 747s and keep their jobs. I felt a bit humble that my sole motivation for the radial keratotomy procedure was just so I could see my audience and fans while I was performing from onstage. Radial keratotomy actually led to the popularity of the modern-day laser surgery. The laser folks need to thank us guinea pigs who put ourselves at risk and under the scalpel. Millions of patients across the globe have benefited and undergone laser eye surgery since our pioneering and experimental surgeries of the late 1980s.

Fyodorov had become one of post-communist Russia's first millionaires. He even made a bid for the Russian presidency in 1996. Fyodorov later died in a helicopter crash in 2000. He was seventy-two. Eventually, a decade after the surgery, radial keratotomy flaws were revealed. The procedure was unstable and some of us who had been nearsighted became farsighted.

In 1991, my father had suffered another stroke, paralysing part of his body. He had a history of medical problems and his health was rapidly deteriorating. It was time for me to return to Australia. A climate of change had altered the landscape of Melbourne, Australia. A severe economic recession was in full swing and there was a sombre mood in the air. Returning home to see the decaying state of my father's health was an inevitable journey I had to make. In retrospect, my emotional bank account and currency of quality time with my father in the last few years was virtually non-existent. A much needed family reunion, irrespective of the dire circumstances was at hand. Konstantinos Halikopoulos, my father, passed away in his sleep on the May 5th, 1993. Determined right to the very last waking hours, he had just finished turning the soil in my mother's much loved and cherished garden, outliving even the most optimistic of doctors' prediction of his impending death by no less than fifteen years of life lived 'to the max'.

To make matters worse, my mother was in Greece when my father died. After much encouragement from the family, she had journeyed back to her homeland for the very first time in forty-five years. My sister Victoria had the most difficult phone call of her life to make. She called her sweetest mother and as gently as possible told her of the grave news. For my mother the great joy of her reunion in Greece with her family and of being with her 101-year-old mother after a four decade absence, was overshadowed by the loss of her soul mate in Australia. My mother fainted in the arms of her older brother. The phone dropped out of her hands and the dial tone was lost. Her youngest brother, a doctor, had her sedated for the return journey to Australia for the funeral.

My grandmother lived to the age of 107. She was one of the oldest women in Europe. She had a strict health regime consisting of red wine, which was rich in anti-oxidants, olive oil, free-range food, clean water, and the clean crisp air of her high mountain retreat.

Upon my arrival in Australia, I became a very popular session guitarist and appeared on many recordings. That same year, I was offered a gig as the lead guitarist with a high profile and popular Melbourne band called Big Deal. What was supposed to be a temporary gig of six months with Big Deal expanded into a decade of touring and recording together. I kept returning to Los Angeles throughout the 1990s whenever I could, and I often wondered if I had stayed there, would my life have turned out any different? Would I have landed the biggest gig in the rock 'n' roll industry?

With Big Deal, we were performing up to six shows per week. The touring was gruelling and I would often get to sleep at 5 am in the morning. We released our original album of material and appeared on several morning and late-night television shows. Big Deal performed with some big name touring acts, such as Bon Jovi and Deep Purple. Coupled with an intense schedule of teaching guitar and doing session work in various recording studios, I was earning a great income. A GIT graduate from Hollywood was in hot demand as a session player and I commanded the appropriate fees. Every aspiring guitarist knew about GIT and with this accreditation, my student base grew to over fifty guitarists eager for me to teach them. Some of these students would later become professional guitarists and launch their own musical careers.

I invested very wisely in residential property during those formative years. These were the early days of the Australian economic recession and the media pundits declared the doomsday and financial catastrophe of property investment. This was at a time when I was studying myself and reading books such as *Think and Grow Rich*, written in the 1930s by Napoleon Hill and *You Were Born Rich* by Bob Proctor, who later became a catalyst in my life. Bob Proctor was my paradigm shift, my true inspiration. I had also read many books by J Paul Getty. He was a 'wildcatter' who drilled for oil in Oklahoma during the 1930s and was one of the first people in the world with a fortune of over one billion dollars. My pursuit of personal development was relentless.

In the book by J Paul Getty, he gave some fantastic advice: When eighty per cent of newspaper sentiment is saying to buy, you should sell. Equally, when eighty per cent of newspaper sentiment is saying to sell, you should buy. In the early days of the Australian recession, when other people were desperately selling property, I was doing the exact opposite. J Paul Getty's creed helped me on the pathway to eternal wealth creation. The media was warning against buying property as an investment and the financial institutions were calling in default loans. By late 1991, I had saved a $50,000 deposit to purchase my first home and borrowed a further $118,000 from the bank. That same property is now worth over $540,000 and fully unencumbered. I originally used that property to leapfrog into a vast property portfolio worth tens of millions of dollars today. I kept acquiring multiple properties each year since 1991, at a rapid rate and have continued to do so ever since. One of my investing secrets was to never sell investment property under any circumstances.

I was quite disciplined in terms of generating cash flow and saving money, especially given the rock 'n' roll lifestyle. Anybody can work and generate money, but the key is to develop multiple pillars of income and find better gainful employment for the money that you do earn. I would get home at 5 am from the gigs and wake up around 10 am. I was operating on four or five hours' sleep. I have never needed much sleep. My philosophy has always been that there's plenty of time for sleep when you're dead. Instead of sleeping in to late afternoon, waking and going to sound check and finding yourself back in another gig a few hours later that night, I used the mornings to search the newspapers for property auctions and inspect properties for pending acquisition.

At the same time, I became a dedicated student of the stock market to capitalise on its massive cash flow benefits. What a contrast – I was a reckless rock musician by night and an astute and savvy investor by day. Soon, I was generating more money in my sleep than when I was awake. It was time for change. Obviously the paradigm of my life was shifting. I was finding it difficult to relate to the musical life on the road and having my life accountable for six nights per week. I was desperate to be the author of my own story and dictate my own circumstances. Life was providing me with the seed of choice. Like a radio that offers new music with each turn of the dial, life was ready to provide me with whatever I was seeking. My thoughts were to act as the tuner for my mind, thus determining the colour of the mental music I would listen to and be influenced by.

This was my discovery phase, my great search for information – a cause, movement or vision that was greater than I was – being exposed to great mentors, authors, embracing distinctions and making conscious decisions with my mental faculty. I had a designated *Hit List* of childhood goals and resolved to do whatever I could to fulfil and be held accountable to them. Life was all about chapters and this transformational phase was the period where I discovered my true purpose. I was ready to take the plunge into full-time investing and take a much needed hiatus from the music industry. Financial prosperity is empowering. If I wanted to visit the cities of Paris, Prague or Marrakech tomorrow, I could. By screening inspiring and imaginative pictures through the movie view finder of my mind, wonderful things started to happen in my life.

THE THRILLIONAIRE® PRINCIPLE

- What is your paradigm shift?
- What is your one true inspiration in life?
- What imaginative pictures are you currently screening through the movie view finder of your mind?

Chapter 5

Bulls and Bedouins

An ounce of action is worth a tonne of theory – Friedrich Engels

After being in the band for over ten years of hardcore touring, five or six nights a week, I really needed a new awakening. I was redefining the screenplay of my life and desperately needed fresh surroundings to launch it. I decided to do something crazy, something daring, and the inspiration – as often happens – was from a movie.

Movies have a fair bit of traction with me. The attraction of films, besides the escapism, is that they often provide metaphors for our lives.

I was watching the comedy movie *City Slickers*. In it Billy Crystal plays a middle-aged guy who has 'lost his smile' and can't seem to find happiness or meaning in his life. So in order to find his *mojo* for life, he sets off with some friends to go on a 'fantasy vacation' where they get to play cowboys on a real cattle drive. Jack Palance plays a crusty old hard-driving cowboy named Curly, guiding the 'city folk' on the drive. Billy Crystal and Jack Palance are having a conversation along the trail.

> Palance asks Crystal,
>
> 'You all come out here about the same age … Same problems … You spend fifty weeks a year getting knots in your rope … You think two weeks up here will untie them for you … None of you get it … Do you know what the secret of life is?'

Crystal responds,

'No, what?'

Palance holds up his gloved index finger and says,

'This.'

Crystal wisecracks,

'Your finger? Your finger is the secret of life?'

Palance continues,

'One thing. Just one thing. You stick to that and everything else don't mean @#*$!'

Crystal asks,

'That's great, but what's the one thing?'

Then Palance gives Crystal the nugget of wisdom he wants him to pay attention to.

'That's what you've gotta figure out.'

I came out of the screening of *City Slickers* and was in deep thought on the way back home. How to reinstate one's magic charm and discover that *One Thing*. I could relate to Billy Crystal's character searching for his *One Thing*, having lost my own smile and searching for more meaning and purpose in my life. Particular scripts of a movie act as metaphors that allow you to evaluate the dramas, dilemmas and realities of your own life. Hence the change of direction in my life and well-needed intermission to restore the balance in my life. I desperately needed to unplug myself from the confines of the system. At this stage of my life, I was financially independent and my savvy investments and wealth strategies were generating more money for me while I was asleep than what I was earning performing as a musician. The problem was, I was lacking inner satisfaction and wanted to feel alive as my passion for music and life had become extinguished.

City Slickers also had another memorable opening scene featuring Billy Crystal and his pals participating in the 'Running of the Bulls' festivity in the Spanish city of Pamplona. That scene stuck with me – the Running of the Bulls during the San Fermin festival seemed an appropriate activity to aerate my soul and ventilate my mindset.

It was thanks to the writing of American writer Ernest Hemingway that the San Fermin festival developed the notoriety of today. The publication of his novel *The Sun Also Rises* in 1926 showed the world the Pamplona bull-running event which attracted people from all over the world to this annual festival. The 'encierro' or the Running of the Bulls is the single most widely-known event of the Fiesta of San Fermin. It is the most extraordinary event which has given the fiesta world-wide fame and which is broadcast around the world. Participants of the fiesta run alongside and in front of ferocious bulls to lead them from their pen up and into the bull-ring. The dangers of running in front of a bull weighing upwards of about 700 kilograms and which has two hard, sharp horns which can pierce and cut into human tissue was something I needed to experience.

The gods were on my side. When I booked my flight to Spain, I had two weeks of lead-up time to the San Fermin festival. This was ideal as I could perform my farewell gig in Australia and make my final exodus. But, on my last gig, that last night, I found it difficult to leave the stage. I just wanted that night to never end, and we played our music till we couldn't play anymore. Afterwards we sat back in the band room, hugged each other and reminisced about our time together. When it was over, it really was over. Next day I packed my bags and, as they say in the westerns, I 'got the hell out of Dodge'. There was no point in waiting around.

I just needed to vacate Melbourne and travel overseas for a six-month trek. That final gig was also the last time I saw most of the guys in the band. The music days were a fun chapter of my life, but I felt there was plenty I was missing out on. The commitment to the band meant we were so accountable in our movements that we virtually had to surrender our social and private lives. We couldn't even organise holidays without everyone having to go on vacation at the same time. I can even recall touring on the night of my brother's wedding.

I made it to the church briefly, but had to leave before the wedding reception to perform a gig. After ten years being a slave to routine, the Running of the Bulls looked like an ideal way to shed the shackles of reason and place my trust in intuition. For me, an adrenalin rush would be a way of defining my mindset – I wanted to stimulate my thought patterns and seek new thrills.

Pamplona stages its week-long San Fermin carnival starting in the first week of July. I caught up with friends and travelled by train from Barcelona to Pamplona and walked from hotel to hotel, looking for somewhere to sleep. Naturally, the town was fully booked. So, we dumped our gear at the railway station, strolled into town and joined up with the festivities. We partied hard. It wasn't a bad effort, really, considering we were carrying our sleeping bags and day packs on our backs.

We weren't worried that we had nowhere to sleep. We were in Europe, and we were having fun. It was just great to escape the protocol and do as we pleased.

Around 6 am, when the partying died down a little, we found a very convenient place for a snooze.

Such is the popularity of the event that overcrowding is a serious problem and if you're planning on staying there, then you should book accommodation many months in advance. Something we discovered first hand when we were forced to roll out our sleeping bags and sleep in an ATM bank cubicle only to be awoken by a drug deal with a local and some drunken tourists. A man selling them cannabis gave us our 'early morning wakeup call'. We needed to get up anyway, because we had some bull running to do. Seeing as we were under the weather, and carrying our backpacks, we weren't exactly in the finest condition for a run that often turns into a race of life and death. The bulls are released from the corral at San Domingo at eight o'clock every morning and they hurtle along the narrow walled streets from one point to another. There are a number of fighting bulls and two herds of bullocks, all of which run 825 metres until they enter the Plaza de Toro, Pamplona's famed bullring. It's a tradition that dates back to the 14th century. This dangerous race, which is run every morning between the seventh and fourteenth of July, starts with a rocket blasting off at the moment the bulls are let out into the street. A second rocket goes off to let everyone know that all the bulls are now in the street.

First of all we climb up Santo Domingo and go across the Ayuntamiento Square continuing down Mercaderes avenue. The most dangerous part of the bull run approaches as there's a closed curve leading into Estafeta avenue which is the longest stretch of the run. Next comes a small section of Duque de Ahumada avenue which is known as the Telefónica stretch. The last stretch is also very risky as the route leads into a dead end street providing access to the bullring.

My friends and I had just arrived. We were naive about the protocol and strategies of the run. It wasn't until the following day that we studied the bull run and the logistics. Foreigners, being foreigners, usually want to start near where the bulls are released. They want to see the bulls when they take-off. It's more exciting.

The locals are shrewder. They have a few hundred years of history that tells them it isn't so smart to run where the bulls are freshest. The local lads usually start their run a couple of hundred metres before the bulls enter the Plaza. They might run only 200 metres, but it's the bit that matters. By that stage, the foreigners are either exhausted or have been mauled or quite possibly killed. The foreigners get the excitement; the locals get the glory.

There's a lot of bravado in the Running of the Bulls, and we were full of that daredevil spirit on the first morning. We wanted to be there when the bulls took off.

The run starts right on 8 am with the firing of rocket. The second explosion sends hearts racing – it tells the runners to get cracking, because each 750 kilogram mass of bull meat and muscle is coming hurtling through the streets. In fact twenty tonnes of sirloin steak is unleashed at this point. Your adrenalin level doubles and your heart rate triples. The excitement and danger releases a torrent of chemicals that give you a massive primeval high. It's an awesome feeling when you hear the rumbling of the hooves thundering towards you on the cobblestones. I could literally hear the earth shuddering as the bulls approached.

Our first run was unforgettable – from start to finish it last precisely eight seconds.

Eight seconds of bull running glory. We sighted the bulls and ran madly. But, in our panic, we both slipped and fell. There was so much glass from broken beer bottles, and jagged edges on the cobbles, that we both ended up with cuts and abrasions.

Still, we were lucky, over fifteen people have died since 1924 and over 200 have been seriously injured.

It would be fair to say that – in that first run – we were not quite in the zone. Not only were we hung over from the partying, but we were carrying backpacks with ten to fifteen kilograms of camera gear and precious items. When we attempted to get up after falling, we kept slipping. We realised it's not the bulls you need to worry about in the Running of the Bulls, it's the other runners. If a runner ahead of you slips, you're over too. With about 5,000 runners sprinting madly down those winding streets, the place is mayhem. We decided that we would do better next day.

The atmosphere of Pamplona in festival week is exhilarating. The town's daily newspaper gets right into the spirit. The first half of the paper is dedicated to the bulls. They get profiled as if they are football players in a big final, or athletes about to compete in the Olympic Games. The life story of each bull is told. We learn who the bull's parents are, where the bull was raised, what are its likes and dislikes. I didn't realise bulls were so interesting.

So after realising that the bulls were at their wildest and freshest at the top of their run, this was deemed too dangerous a location to begin the run. That, obviously, is the worst place to be when you're a runner. If you intend to survive, let the foreigners run with the bulls, and then come in with the Spaniards a couple of hundred metres from the Plaza de Toro coliseum when the bulls have let off most of their steam. We spoke to locals about their favourite places, and most recommended joining in at a turn called Curva de Mercaderes hacia Estafeta. It's a very sharp bend but – if you get around it – you've got a long, straight run to the bullring. Two important things have to be kept in mind at this point: it's very dangerous to take the turn on the wide side, that's to say, on the left side. The bulls, carried by their own inertia, tend to pull over towards the left and they slide up against the fence and the wall on the corner. They sometimes lose their footing and anyone caught between the wall and the bull could get flattened by them or even suffer some more serious misfortune. So our Spanish colleagues commanded us to take this turn on the right side. This was like insider trading information, useful nevertheless.

Once the bulls and surviving runners are in the Plaza de Toro, the gates are shut.

The runners struggling along behind the bulls are locked out – even if they have just run the full journey from when the bulls were released. The poor foreigners generally have no chance of making it to the coliseum where the matadors are introduced to the arena like gladiators, ready to do battle with the bulls. The runners also have little chance of going home unscathed. We found that the spectators viewing the run have a very gladiatorial attitude to the entertainment. When a runner jumps the fence to escape the mayhem, the locals throw them back onto the cobbled street. If the runner is bleeding, or has an injury, or is seeking medical attention, they just applaud and keep throwing them back. It's a blood sport. There's not a lot of logic to it, but that's Pamplona. If you want logic, go to Paris or Prague or Princeton. Don't go to Pamplona.

On the second morning we started with the locals. We had a fantastic run and made it into the Plaza. We even took the opportunity to slap the bulls on the rump, as the locals do. We witnessed quite a few injuries, where bulls that had become separated from the main group attacked and gored runners. But there were no fatalities. Still, it was a blast of craziness – just what I needed to shake me out of my comfort zone and rediscover my edge.

Since I was there, the run has become more civilised. Back then, you just showed up in your white shirt and red scarf, and ran as hard as you could. Now runners have to qualify in tests of their fitness and preparedness. When I ran, there were plenty who were overweight and intoxicated, and some of them should have been sleeping it off, rather than putting themselves at risk. It makes sense that the authorities are clamping down.

After we had satisfied ourselves of all that Pamplona had to offer, we roamed

Spain and then I finally made my way to Morocco in North Africa. This trip for me was an exodus from my former life. I had the luxury of time and finance, and I was looking for an even more invigorated direction. My goal when I left the band was to become a full-time investor, but I knew the hardest part would be to break out of the late-night club routine. When you're involved in the music industry, you become institutionalised. Every night of the week is accounted for. To find the smile on my face I had to become disconnected from the band. I no longer wanted to be responsible for anyone else's plans, or for their ability to earn a livelihood. I wanted to fly solo.

The trip to Europe and North Africa enabled me to do things I'd always wanted, and one of them was to experience the desert sands of Morocco. From as far back as I can remember, I have always been fascinated with the Bedouin culture of the Saharan region of Morocco. The word 'Bedouin' comes from the Arab word 'Bedou' that means 'Desert Dweller.' Whilst travelling in Morocco, North Africa, I enquired about making contact with Bedouin local tribesmen in Marrakech to seek desert passage under their guidance. Having been told by friends in Marrakech that I could travel with them in return for purchasing some livestock for them I was thrilled that I could literally hitch a ride and spend up to the next fortnight in the desert with them. Experiencing the desert sands of the Sahara with native Bedouins – and the opportunity of spending nights in a genuine Bedouin tent, trekking across the dunes on a camel and drinking mint tea with the locals was a divine invitation I would never forget.

I've been fascinated by North Africa since I was a young boy, viewing movies about the French Foreign Legion and the mystique of the North African deserts. In Marrakech, a city at the foothills of the Atlas Mountains, we roamed around the medieval part, visiting the kasbahs and medinas. It was like stepping back a thousand years in time. Wherever you go, you see poets, prophets, snake charmers, sabre-rattling theatricals, trained monkeys and fire-eaters. It's such a quirky, colourful sideshow of a city. How can you not fall under Morocco's spell?

The Bedouin lifestyle is generally nomadic and pastoral, consisting of herding camels, sheep, goats and cattle. Bedouins migrate according to the seasons, travelling where the grazing conditions are best. In winter, when there is some water about, they roam deeper into the desert. In hot, dry summers, they camp around secure water sources. Bedouins define themselves as members of tribes and families. They are divided into social classes, depending on ancestry and profession. What a contradiction their culture is to the 'rock star' lifestyle I had left behind. I really wanted to experience a simple existence, where the only quest that truly matters is the search for water.

I was told I could pay for passage on their caravan through a barter type system – perhaps by purchasing some livestock, perhaps a goat, or maybe a bag of wheat or flour. Bedouins don't have a monetary system. Their currency is food or clothing or whatever can help sustain them. When they agreed to take me along, it was a real eye-opener to travel with these traditional nomadic dwellers who roam the desert in search of water wells. I packed lightly – a sleeping bag and a few clothes were all I would carry – and I left the rest of my backpack in Marrakech.

The Bedouins I encountered were extremely friendly and accommodating to me and welcomed me into their lives. They were from the Tuareg desert tribe. The most striking feature of the Tuaregs is that they wear blue scarves as veils to cover their heads and faces, leaving only their eyes exposed. Tuareg men believe it is impolite for their mouths or noses to be seen. The dyed indigo blue scarves are six or seven metres long, and they wind the scarves loosely around their heads and faces.

Because temperatures in the desert can climb to 48 °C, or 120 °F, during daylight, layering the fabric adds insulation from the heat and extra protection against the sand, which finds its way into everything. The caravan I travelled with into the scorching desert consisted of about fifteen camels and twenty-eight tribal members.

My transportation into the scorching desert for the next fourteen days was to be a camel. The camels really were giants of the desert – they stand over 1.85 m tall at the shoulder and 2.15 m at the hump. Getting on or off a camel is no easy task. They first get up on their hind legs, which almost throws you over the front of the camel. As for speed, they're surprisingly quick. They can run up to sixty kilometres per hour in short bursts and sustain speeds of forty kilometres per hour. As we rode our 'ships of the desert', I felt like Lawrence of Arabia, the legendary World War One British officer who fought alongside Arab troops under the command of Emir Faisal in guerrilla operations against the armed forces of the Ottoman Empire.

The Tuareg tribe had tents made from worsted fibre. Their cuisine was mostly couscous, with lots of rice and some goat meat. They killed goats for food as they went along, storing food and excess materials in caves. Each day we travelled about fifteen kilometres, stopping at wells to make camp. None of my hosts spoke proper English, so my communication with them was stilted. I had fifty to sixty words of the Tuareg dialect written down on a sheet of paper, mostly the fundamental words such as water, food and sleep.

Despite the language barrier, we seemed to understand each other quite well. They were very patient with me and they were easy to travel with. Their faces were lined and leathery from the harsh climate and their daily grind was gruelling, but they were gentle people to be amongst. In two weeks, I didn't hear of one argument. They just rode their camels and walked and rode their camels some more. Every morning at daybreak they packed up their swags, had a bit of breakfast, and got started on the day's journey. Breakfast was a drink of goat's milk and a piece of bread, or some meat or rice. At night, they sat around a campfire, reciting poetry and telling stories. They carted shrub and bush with them to light their campfires. Many of the Arabs and Berbers in the tribes have not altered their lifestyles for centuries, still following the traditions of their respective cultures.

As we ventured into the Sahara Desert, the vastness of it overwhelmed me. The Sahara stretches from the Atlantic Ocean to the Red Sea, and up and down the extent of North Africa. The desert is often flat and appears to be barren with many small rocks. The conventional image of rolling sand dunes does exist, but further into the interior. Here the Sahara exceeds every single hope and expectation. I imagine that the sheer size of the sand dunes would be a very humbling experience for many first-time travellers to these exotic parts. A full moon over the desert night is unforgettable, as well as sunrises and sunsets, both of which are famous in the Sahara because of their magnificence and luminescence.

As we made our way towards Merzouga and Erfoud, we encountered other ancient nomadic tribes. Merzouga is best described as an oasis area. This is one of the few places in the desert where water can be found in wells – making it an obvious choice for a settlement. As we headed across the desert to our settlement each night, I was reminded how unforgiving the desert can be – even for a camel that doesn't find it's way back to the water well. The skeletal remains of animals litter the desert.

As we approached a mud hut with a wooden-beamed roof, I found a woman sitting in the shade next to some clay pots. Believe it or not, her home had solar panels to generate electricity for lights and a television set.

I also noticed that the Bedouin women were duty bound to carry water from the well to their camp, and in most cases, women had to travel several kilometres in the scorching heat. Meanwhile, the men passed the evenings by trading news and discussing their animals. Separated from the men by a curtain, the women gathered in the family area and kitchen to bake bread and prepare the main meal. When we finished dinner, a bonfire was built and we were treated to ancient Berber music under the stars. The ritual was repeated every evening. As there are no formal mosques in the desert, the Tuaregs pray where they are, facing Mecca and performing the ritual washing, preferably with water. Since water is not always available in the desert, I witnessed them wash with sand. I later discovered that Islam's prophet Mohammed was born and raised in the Bedouin tribe of the Quraish. The Qur'an, first revealed to Mohammed, was later written and compiled in the Arabic language. The first converts to Islam came from Bedouin tribes living in and around the city of Mecca. Islam is therefore deeply embedded in Bedouin culture.

My journey was mostly through the sub-Sahara, towards the coast, across lots of rock and sand formations. As they rode their camels and walked, the adults taught their kids how to read the land, the water, the wells and the weather. I daresay that knowledge had been passed down for generations. Experiencing the desert sands of the Sahara, having the opportunity to spend nights in a genuine Bedouin tent, trekking across the dunes on a camel and drinking mint tea with the tribes-people was a divine experience I would never forget. I was privileged to gain acceptance into that tribe. A few months before, I had been living at the height of hedonism – in the music industry. Ten years on, I don't know if their lifestyle has been eroded – they might well be driving vans, for all I know. Many other Bedouins in the Middle East left their traditional nomadic lives in the 1950s and 1960s, but the Tuareg seemed steadfast and content roaming as their forebears had for thousands of years.

I ended the last morning of my Bedouin experience with a camel trek to see a fantastic sunrise over the dunes. I was mesmerised by the clarity of colours, and the experience left me enriched with a more defined sense of purpose. I was stripped back to basics and had temporarily lived the life of a nomad, with plenty of time to think, reflect and resurface with a renewed enthusiasm for the possibilities of life. I left my new friends in the desert after being invigorated by their presence, having been nurtured by their ancient culture, ageless principles and timeless techniques equipped to liberate the potential of the mind, body and soul.

THE THRILLIONAIRE® PRINCIPLE

- Have you discovered that One Thing in your life?
- What facets of life are you most fascinated with?
- Have you ever reflected and resurfaced with a renewed enthusiasm for the possibilities of your life?

Chapter 6

Evolutionary psychology

The richest place in the world is the graveyard of all the dreams that were never fulfilled. In life we have to fight for our dreams, otherwise unfulfilled dreams have a habit of haunting us for the rest of our lives – Nik Halik

With everything we do in our lives, we need to resonate in harmonic vibration with our core beliefs and values, so that we can achieve what we desire. As I travel the globe, I often get asked about the secrets of success and financial prosperity. People want to know how I can assist them in discovering financial freedom. My response is that I can educate them with an array of wealth pillars, but this only comprises about one per cent of the equation. Ninety nine per cent is the psychological attribute. It's a way of freedom. Quite simply, it's about unlocking your potential. I was born rich, rich in human potential. I was certainly not born into wealth. I had to discover the formula to wealth prosperity on my own by embracing a myriad of strategies. My personal goal each year is to set sail on a new paradigm and continually be in the orbit of the most influential minds on the planet. Hence the evolution of the mind that is paramount here.

There are tribes in the Amazon where indigenous Indians have lived to a phenomenal age. Some have been reported to be well into their 100s, even as much as 150. Why do they live so long? My belief is that it's because they have never been programmed to die at seventy or eighty the way that people in western society have been. Programming is a powerful and restrictive force in our lives. We've been hard-wired to think in certain ways and to follow patterns set by the system. This works against our own individuality and limits what we can achieve. It certainly restricts us from achieving our dreams. What we all need to do is to delete our old programming.

I use the metaphor of the Parthenon. It has stood for thousands of years because it has a strong foundation and a structure of supportive pillars. The foundation of it is equivalent to your belief system and mindset. If your initial foundation is contaminated, you're attempting to build a financial future on quicksand. This cancerous growth will permeate and spread its tentacles if left unchecked.

If you want to erect a skyscraper, you must ensure your mindset and foundations are solid. Your goal is to build a solid base, on which to erect financial pillars. Most people who've been to Italy have been to Pisa, a city in Tuscany to visit a very famous leaning tower. Why is it called the Leaning Tower of Pisa? Most people think the answer is because of its defective structural engineering. The real truth is that the soil in its base was contaminated with unstable subsoil that allowed the foundation to shift direction. Hence, the design was flawed from the beginning. For hundreds of years, in an effort to compensate for the tilt, engineers built higher-angled floors with one side taller than the other to allow the tower to lean in the other direction. A multinational task force of engineers, mathematicians and historians over the past 800 years were assigned to save it from collapsing. What they all failed to realise was the importance of the subsoil foundation in the first instance. What does this metaphor share with the initial setting of the thermostat and the foundation of our life?

The Leaning Tower of Pisa still remains a marvel, but you don't want to build your financial future on shaky foundations. We need to have a solid blueprint and firm foundations as early as possible to avoid financial cancer, thus ensuring a wave of financial prosperity. Our blueprint is like a thermostat. By continually resetting the thermostat, we reset our minds and install an *AntiVirus* protection program for the mind. The unfortunate reality is that we fail to believe in ourselves and in our own ability to think. We doubt our ability to create, and our ability to achieve. If we don't believe in ourselves, we lack accountability.

A desert becomes a forest with the right gardener. Imagine a tree of life. The tree of life is an important symbol in nearly every culture, with its branches reaching into the sky, and roots deep in the soil of the earth. An eternal tree of life bears fruit. In life, our fruits are the equivalent of our manifested results. So, what does humanity tend to do? Most place too much attention and focus on the fruits, the monetary results. But it's the seeds and the roots that create the ripeness of those fruits. It's what's under the ground that is the secret garden, and the nurturing of the soil that creates what is above the ground. It's the hidden gem, the invisible component that manifests the visible results in our life. What you cannot see in this world is far more powerful than anything that you can see. This garden analogy proves to be the fertile reasoning in giving birth to some of life's most valuable lessons. Just as seeds in a garden require sun, water, and soil to thrive, the seeds of positive thought require adequate nurturing in the form of discipline and a belief system. By transforming the composition of the fruits, you first have to transform the roots. If you want to change the visible, you must first change the invisible.

With regards to our foundation and blueprint, we need to define our 'why' in life which provides our sense of purpose. This neural networking and modelling process provides the reasoning or catalyst for change. When we have a powerful vision, we bend the universe to our will. An individual without a 'why' is a ship without a rudder. No matter how hard you attempt to sail the rudderless ship, it goes nowhere. It just churns water, totally ineffectively. Once we formulate our 'why', every action in our life takes on a more definite meaning. From that moment forwards, every action etched in our minds manifests itself in reality towards our goals. I was very fortunate to experience this paradigm shift of thinking, even though – at the time – I didn't even know what a paradigm was.

If you were to sit down and have somebody read the eulogy of your life upon your passing, what would you like to hear? A eulogy personalised about your life could be the toughest speech you'll ever be forced to listen to. What would the overall theme convey? What legacy did you leave behind that will enable others to find strength from. Most people in life have only a vague idea and most often there is no real direction in their life. This is when the reading of the eulogy takes a dramatic turn. Would you ask for one more chance and more time to prove yourself? What would you do differently if you had more time?

What are some tasks you would definitely commit to if you were granted more time? What would you be willing to do, just for another hour of life, another day or perhaps even an extra year? Assuming you have the life you desire from this moment on, what will your eulogy say about your life?

Your goal needs to be something tangible that is real or physical. If your goals do not inspire you, it is unrealistic to expect that you will be driven to take action to achieve them. For every goal and ambition you have selected into your future timeline, you need to ask yourself the following questions: *Is what I'm doing right now moving me towards or away from my goals?* By being definite, you can conduct a daily stocktake of your life. Ask yourself, *Have I discovered something new?* You'll notice that I use the words *discover* quite often. I'm careful not to use the word *learn*. I feel the word is too closely associated with the academic schooling system and can be considered by many people to be negative. The schooling system is such an irrelevant institution in its current format. *Learn* is not a word I want to perpetuate here. Discovery is all about empowerment and the DNA of our soul. The soul of your DNA is the composition of your dreams, destiny lived, conscious and unconscious. It is made of your past, your successes and especially your failures. This discovery phase reinforces the need to harness new energies and opportunities in our lives – just like the exploration of new frontiers in space.

Daily life should always consist of embracing new distinctions of change and an optimised set of higher values. This process validates your thinking faculty. Most people who are trapped with an institutionalised mindset fail to think for themselves. They've lost their faculty of thinking and have simply become a warehouse of facts. I personally believe that many institutionalised people are lucky enough to think twice a year. In many cases, people only tend to think in times of emergency. In normal life, they haven't raised their level of awareness to what's around them. They have become slaves to a program of conventional thought installed from birth, slaves to something called, the 'System'. Let's expand our minds here with your permission. Imagine a world where a System runs a program-generated virtual environment specifically designed to control people. The inhabitants of this hallucinatory world choose to believe that everything is real. But what if they were really floating in pod-like vats hooked up to a manufactured colony of thought patterns. What if they were no different to 'batteries' and purposely drained for energy while keeping them entranced and powerless.

This System of thought has programmed their mindset. Their free thought has been commandeered to the extent that they are no longer able to probe questions or challenge the status quo. Programming occurs everywhere – from the moment we go to school, from the moment we join the workforce. Switch on the news, or pick up a newspaper, and you'll see the parameters of the System set by those who rule the System. Most people don't challenge themselves enough to see the System for what it is. Unfortunately, most of humanity has been programmed to have one job or source of income. Why? It serves the System. What better way for the shepherd being the System to control and sedate the flock. Allow me to explain. Having one source of income and servicing your life with after tax dollars is a sure-fire recipe to being dead broke. Now combine this thought with the fact that you were purposely denied financial education whilst at school, in order to keep you financially ignorant. Think about it, were you ever educated about money at school? The result is that up to ninety-five per cent of the working population works by necessity. The definition of necessity is doing whatever it takes in order to survive. Individuals across the globe are disconnected and remain subservient to the System.

When you look at the morning commute to get to work, most individuals are grinding away out of the necessity to do so. *The reality is you're working hard enough at work so you don't get sacked, while the employer pays you just enough so you don't quit.* A well-worn path isn't necessarily the right path to take in life. Humanity has been programmed to negate inner feelings and to work for the System.

The System reprimands dreamers. When you speak to kids, they have the most vivid dreams. They want to see the world, become a fireman or travel to the moon. Why is it that in adult life we no longer have those dreams, or that we block ourselves from achieving those childhood dreams? The short answer is that we have allowed the System to institutionalise our mindset and take hold of us, hence becoming servants of that System – as opposed to making the System a servant of us. We must become an architect of our own life and become the lighthouse of influence that illuminates our family and friends.

This System was never designed for the people or to look after us. It was designed to maintain the status quo and strengthen the institutional financial power brokers. Workers are always sent the bill and pay for everything. If there is some kind of disaster we pay for it. The System is designed to spit out just enough cash to keep us just above what is regarded as the revolution level, where you are not out in the street burning and tearing the System apart.

In fact people who wear 'suits' might get disgruntled with me for making this observation, but why else besides necessity would a man wear something as restrictive as a tie? It's a piece of cloth strung around your neck. It's a badge of the System. Of course, there may be people who wear ties because they like them, or because they're going to functions, or they want to fit in, but who would wear a suit and tie to work in particular if they didn't have to? All these office workers wearing suits and ties – do they wear them by choice or necessity? And there are the self- employed business owners. So many self-employed people think they are not ruled by necessity, and that they run their own business. When you take a closer examination though, most self-employed people have purchased a job and become a slave to it. They just get to pay themselves last. Most self-employed people work *in* the job rather than *on* it. Working in the job means that your business relies on your physical presence to be able to generate cash flow. So in summary, most people working in their own business simply have bought themselves a job, work longer hours, carry all the responsibility and pay themselves last.

I have utilised the opportunities given to me in my life and have strived to build the pillars of spiritual, psychological, physical and monetary health on a solid foundation.

Much of life is about a mindset. We all have the choice of who we are, and what we represent. It's an old saying but it's true: *you are who you associate with.*

As a young man, attempting to find my path in the world, I always networked with individuals or groups who were transmitting a frequency of greater wisdom. I aspired to embrace their mindset. My belief is that you either choose to walk through a new door of enlightenment or that door will be closed to you for the rest of your life. Unless you experience change and adopt higher values, the System will dominate our lives.

I'll give you an example. If you go to your local railway station and board a morning train to the city, more often than not, you'll sit next to a person who may be expressionless and glum. But, if you engage that person in a conversation and allow them to describe their favourite hobby, I bet they'll glow. Life will come into their faces. They suddenly feel happy and animated. The hobby is what provides the exuberance in their life. My question is: *Why can't people pursue their hobby, do what makes them happy, all the time? Why doesn't their hobby become their job?* Why not make investing your perpetual hobby once you've acquired the necessary financial skills. Napoleon Hill, in his book *Think and Grow Rich* said, 'Action is the real measure of intelligence'. Thomas Huxley, in *Aphorisms and Reflections*, said, 'The great end of life is not knowledge but action.'

Ask yourself these questions: *What thinking can I take on board in order to manifest the changes in my life? What can I do right now in order to change the path of my life? How can I challenge the status quo to take on new challenges? How can I generate more cash flow in my life?*

An interesting facet in order for change must encompass positive language patterns. The words *one day, try, wish, hope* and *can't* are by far the most disempowering words we are guilty of using in our vocabulary. In relation to the *one day* statement, Confucius said, 'Man shoot at nothing, sure to hit it.' Think of this, if an individual is not aiming at anything in particular, they will have amazing accuracy at achieving it. By remaining date specific and endorsing positive language patterns we maintain accountability to our thoughts and actions. *Wish* and *hope* are words resonating in a negative vibration. Why *wish* or *hope* when you can strive for and create actionable steps to achieving success. The word *try* is essentially a failure disease. There is no such thing as *try*. We either make the conscious decision to do something or simply choose not to. Jedi Master Yoda from *Star Wars: Episode V – The Empire Strikes Back* (1980) contains a memorable line relating to the negative language of *trying*. This particular scene takes place in the swamp land of the planet Dagobah, where a young Luke Skywalker is studying the Force under the training of Jedi Master Yoda.

> Jedi Master Yoda: 'For my ally is the Force, and a powerful ally it is. Life creates it, makes it grow. Its energy surrounds us and binds us. Luminous beings are we, not this crude matter. You must feel the Force around you.'
>
> Luke Skywalker: 'All right, I'll give it a try.'
>
> Jedi Master Yoda: 'No. Try not. Do ... or do not. There is no try.'
>
> Using the Force, Yoda effortlessly frees the X-Wing spacecraft from the swamp.
>
> Luke Skywalker: 'I don't, I don't believe it.'
>
> Jedi Master Yoda: 'That is why you fail.'

By using a filtering process, we can also start to set the parameters as to who we invite into our lives. You can highlight who you desire to associate with. If people are negative, you can simply avoid them. Associate with individuals who enlighten you. Similar to a car's filtering system. What does it do? It removes impurities. Life works similarly for people. The human mind is the world's largest filtering device. We all have negative people in our lives, those who hold us back, or frustrate us. Negative friends will never want you to change. They want to hold you back where they are. Misery requires company. Never allow their misery to engulf your life. Your choice is to avoid those people and become a beacon of light for others to follow. By nurturing weary souls searching for a lighthouse, you will keep them from crashing against the rocky shores. You can illuminate, enlighten and enrol them into your dream.

It all begins with a belief system and a readiness to change. Unless a student is ready, the teacher will never arrive. For most people, the path to discovery and answers, are already there. It's just a matter of defining where that path is, and how to follow it. We just need to vaccinate ourselves against 'excusitis'. Everyone has their 'pot of gold' or preferred choice of destination, in regards to what they aspire to accomplish in life. It's a matter of finding it. We need to make the paths so vivid that we can find them.

Unfortunately most people live in a dim world. You can have a 'pot of gold' that is just a few metres away, yet – if your 'pot of gold' is dim – there's no way you'll find it. How do you light up your path? The simple answer is by undergoing a metamorphosis. I wouldn't say you need to have a light bulb moment; rather you need to have halogen moments of certainty. Once you have certainty, you begin to accept more. Certainty removes fear. What do most people fear in life? They fear the unknown. How do you achieve certainty? By being definitive in everything you do in life. By defining your 'why' and doing whatever it takes to achieve that 'why'. That phrase *whatever it takes* is paramount here. You really do need to give all your mental energy to making this change. Every day people should ask themselves the following: *When was the last time I did something for the very first time? When was the last time I viewed a new vantage point in life?* If you probe that question carefully, you'll probably find that you've done the same thing over and over again. That is called the law of diminishing intent. It's doing the same thing over and over again, but expecting a different outcome. If we're not willing to embrace new thoughts and experiences, effectively we're procrastinating.

Procrastination is a fear fertiliser. By fertilising our fears and negativity, we proceed to justify why we've chosen not to change. We have a choice to alter our state of mind, or we can choose to stay idle. In life, nothing around us stays the same. If we don't progress, by law we naturally regress. My suggestion is to list all the negative aspects of your life on one board. On a different board, list all the positive aspects of your life. It's a stocktake of your life – spiritually, emotionally, physically and monetarily. As an International Wealth Strategist and Educator, whenever I take someone on as a client, I always insist they encourage, enlighten and nurture someone else to join them on their journey.

Kaizen is a Japanese word which means a continuous and incremental improvement of a person's life. Kaizen involves taking small-action steps over time to solve problems. The beauty of this approach lies within its simplicity. You begin something that initially seems daunting, but in fact, it is the small easy step that helps you bypass the feelings of fear. If we procrastinate we fertilise more fear. If we commit ourselves to the successful completion of a task, then we personify excellence. By simply introducing another small step and another, we jettison the confines of our comfort zone and relish in the power of self-examination.

I recall a musical in London starring Sir Laurence Olivier which featured in the 1960s. The musical was named *Time*, and Sir Laurence Olivier played the character of the Time Lord. I was given the soundtrack of this famous excerpt ten years ago and forever absorbed every magical word. The premise was that we all possess a powerful key for the application of change in our lives.

> Stand before me on the sign of infinity, all you of the earth. With the granting of the law of provination comes the application of change. I will give you the key. And with this knowledge, please realise, comes the responsibility of sharing it. I will show you the way. It's very simple. Throughout the universe there is order. In the movement of the planets, in nature and in the functioning of the human mind. A mind that is in its natural state of order is in harmony with the universe and such a mind is timeless. Your life is an expression of your mind. You are the creator of your own universe – for as a human being, you are free to will whatever state of being you desire through the use of your thoughts and words. There is great power there. It can be a blessing or a curse – it's entirely up to you. For the quality of your life is brought about by the quality of your thinking – think about that. Thoughts produce actions – look at what you're thinking. See the pettiness and the envy and the greed and the fear and all the other attitudes that cause you pain and discomfort. Realise that the one thing you have absolute control over is your attitude. See the effect that it has on those around you. For each life is linked to all life and your words carry with them chain reactions like a stone that is thrown into a pond. If your thinking is in order, your words will flow directly from the heart creating ripples of love. If you truly want to change your world, my friends, you must change

> your thinking. Reason is your greatest tool, it creates an atmosphere of understanding, which leads to caring which is love. Choose your words with care. Go forth ... with love.

Most people refuse to confront their own lives, probably because they're intimidated by what they'll find out. We don't have to accept our environment. These days the internet has connected up the world. We're more global but, unfortunately, our societies have grown more disconnected. Now computer games and video games trap our youth and comatose them in the confines of their home, removing them from their families and from the world around them. Once, people walked around their communities, their towns, their countries. Now everyone drives. The motorways are clogged with disconnected people. Communication used to be face-to-face. Now people exist on cell phones and internet chat rooms. When people undertake a serious appraisal and stocktake of their lives, they should approach it with an honest and transparent perspective. We want to reflect back on our lives and respect ourselves. We want to reflect positively on the mosaic of different cultural experiences in our lives. For me, it was the kaleidoscope of different adventures. For you, it could be whatever you desire, whatever response that makes you passionate about your 'why'.

At many wealth conferences across the globe, I often ask individuals a specific question that intrigues me, due to the multiple complexities of responses. I ask them: *Where is the richest place in the world?* Most people incorrectly say Dubai, US, Saudi Arabia ... What do you think my response to them is? '*The richest place in the world is the graveyard of all the dreams that were never fulfilled. In life we have to fight for our dreams, otherwise unfulfilled dreams have a habit of haunting us for the rest of our lives.*' A stunned audience upon hearing this applauds and passionately accepts this reality.

Carpe diem ... seize the day. The definition of this concept was poignantly illustrated in this magical scene in Peter Weir's movie *Dead Poets Society*. The setting is in 1959, at the Welton Academy in Vermont. Welton was an old-fashioned but well-respected private school where education was preached in a rigorous academic learning arena combined with the shaping of traditionalist ideals. In this scene, the school walls are lined with class pictures dating back into the 1800s. School trophies of every description fill trophy cases and shelves. John Keating, the teacher who was their inspiration and made their lives extraordinary, played by Robin Williams, leads the students in, then faces the class.

Keating: 'Gather ye rosebuds while ye may. The Latin term for that sentiment is "carpe diem". Anyone know what that means?'

Meeks: 'Carpe diem … seize the day.'

Keating: 'Very good ... ?'

Meeks: 'Meeks.'

Keating: 'Seize the day while you're young, see that you make use of your time. Why does the poet write these lines?'

A student: 'Because he's in a hurry?'

Keating: 'Because we're food for worms, lads! Because we're only going to experience a limited number of springs, summers, and falls. One day, hard as it is to believe, each and every one of us is going to stop breathing, turn cold, and die! Stand up and peruse the faces of the boys who attended this school sixty or seventy years ago. Don't be timid, go look at them.'

The boys get up and go over to the class pictures that line the honour room walls. Faces of young men stare at them from out of the past.

Keating: 'They're not that different than any of you, are they? There's hope in their eyes, just like in yours. They believe themselves destined for wonderful things, just like many of you. Well, where are those smiles now, boys? What of that hope?'

The boys are staring at the pictures, sobered by what Keating is saying.

Keating: 'Did most of them not wait until it was too late before making their lives into even one iota of what they were capable? In chasing the almighty deity of success did they not squander their boyhood dreams? Most of those gentlemen are fertilising daffodils! However, if you get very close, boys, you can hear them whisper. Go ahead, lean in, hear it? (Loud whisper) Carpe diem, lads. Seize the day. Make your lives extraordinary.'

THE THRILLIONAIRE® PRINCIPLE

- With regards to the foundation and blueprint of your life, define your 'why'?
- How can you challenge the status quo to take on new challenges?
- What would you like to hear in your eulogy?

Chapter 7

Space exploration

The motherland hears, the motherland knows where her son flies in the sky – from the patriotic song by Dmitri Shostakovich and Yevgeniy Dolmatovsky

YOU'RE LOCKED IN, STRAPPED TIGHT AND READY FOR THE MOST breathtaking ride of your life. The pilot is in a cockpit that's separate from you – above and behind where you are. So you feel like you're on your own as you look out over the aircraft's nose. You're thinking just how incredibly powerful this jet is. The statistics are mind-boggling. This modified aircraft can generate 30,000 pounds of thrust. It can reach speeds faster than Mach 3 (three times the speed of sound, 3,000 kilometres per hour or one mile every two seconds) and it can climb up to 125,000 feet. In a matter of minutes, you'll be at an altitude more than three times higher than Mt Everest. How can you relate that to any experience you've ever had before? Passengers in 747 jets fly at a relatively miniscule 36,000 feet. This flight can take you over 90,000 feet higher than you've ever been. The jet aircraft you're sitting in is a MIG 25 jet, an incredibly high-speed interceptor and reconnaissance/bomber jet aircraft designed during the Cold War era by the Soviet Union. It's about to carry you into the skies over Russia – and then into the edge of space.

On that morning in 2003 when I sat in the cockpit of a modified MIG 25, I thought of my father. If only he had been alive to witness my imminent 'edge of space' flight and the turn of events unfolding. Soaring to the 'edge of space' was one of the most exhilarating experiences for me thus far.

In all of human history fewer than 450 people have ever travelled into space. And just twelve men have walked on the moon. It's my ambition to join that exclusive club, and to walk on the lunar landscape. Obviously, space travel is a very difficult field to get into. Only the most qualified and competent professionals are selected to join national space programs. I received my invitation through the only civilian space program in the world – conducted by the Russian Federation at the Yuri Gagarin Cosmonaut Training Centre, outside Moscow.

When I arrived in Russia in 2003, it also happened to be the 856th anniversary of the city of Moscow. Vladimir Putin, the president of Russia wanted the festivities to be prolific and a media showcase to the world. The Russians also hoped for clear blue skies and overall good weather. The problem was that, days prior to the anniversary festivities, it was raining continuously. While watching the Russian evening news in my hotel suite, a news correspondent reported that Vladimir Putin deployed the air force to seed incoming clouds so they rained over Finland instead. Silver iodide flares were ignited and dispersed as the air force jets rocketed through cumulus clouds, manipulating them in the direction of Finland instead. These experimental and secretive flights managed to halt the rain for the weekend, clearing the way for two days of blue skies in Moscow. On Monday, after the anniversary, came the rain again. How's that for Russian ingenuity and determination. Other superpowers have unleashed cloud seeding chemicals for their own agenda. In 1969, the Central Intelligence Agency (CIA) was accused of seeding clouds to produce rain at the Woodstock Festival to disrupt its celebrations. The Woodstock Festival exemplified the counterculture of the 1960s and the 'hippie era.' Thirty-two of the best-known musicians of this time period appeared during the rainy weekend. Members of the hippy revolution and movement at the time claimed to have witnessed clouds being seeded by the US military. This was said to be the cause of the rain which lasted throughout the festival.

The Yuri Gagarin Cosmonaut Training Centre was named after Yuri Gagarin. Yuri Gagarin was a Hero of the Soviet Union and a Soviet cosmonaut. On April 12th, 1961, Gagarin became the first human to travel into space in Vostok 3KA-2. Gagarin is immortalised across the world and still remains a national icon in Russia. On March 27th, 1968, he and his instructor mysteriously died in a MIG 15UTI on a routine training flight near Kirzhach. Yuri was certainly one of my mentors. In fact my father gave me a poster of him to put up on my bedroom wall when I was a young child.

At the Yuri Gagarin Cosmonaut Training Centre, selected civilians are sometimes given the opportunity to train alongside Russian cosmonauts and NASA astronauts. An astronaut or cosmonaut is a person trained by a human spaceflight program to command, pilot, or serve as a crew member of a spacecraft. The full program at the Star City cosmonaut facility consists of edge of space, suborbital, zero gravity flights, vestibular training, neutral buoyancy training and even survival training in Siberia. The reason why the Russian government runs a civilian passenger program is because it helps cover some of the costs of their cosmonaut program. The going rate for a trip to the International Space Station (ISS) is currently around $US30 million, so it's obviously a select group who get the privilege of space travel. Besides being wealthy, those who travel to the ISS must pass through the rigorous cosmonaut-training program, where they are expected to meet the highest medical and physical standards.

Yuri Gagarin was one of my father's heroes, and I'll tell you more about both of them later. But first, let me tell you how exhilarating the experience of being in a MIG 25 was. The heightened state of awareness was such that I thought I'd never come back to Earth. The pilot for my flight was Alexander Pavlov, a renowned test pilot at the cosmonaut facility. We had a long chat on the day before my flight, and he gave me an insight into what the Yuri Gagarin Cosmonaut Training Centre meant to him.

He told me his father had lived and died as a test pilot, and that he would be happy to do the same. 'To experience the same fate of my father's would be an honourable climax to my life,' Alex told me. I was impressed by his commitment although, naturally enough, I was seeking reassurance that Alex was planning to remain on Earth for a bit longer yet. I later checked Alex's record and confirmed that his father – Valery Pavlov – was a celebrated Russian test pilot who perished while testing jets in 1994. Alexander and I talked about the fear of the unknown and he said – with total candour – that he had no fear.

As a pilot, he has tested MIG 29s, Su 24s, Su 27s and Su 30s, and is a member of the renowned Test Flight emonstration group, which is headed by Russian hero Anatoly Kvotchur.

When I climbed into the MIG 25, I was sitting in the cockpit with the same full instrumentation as Alex. I couldn't see him from my cockpit, so a couple of times during flight – when the silence seemed a bit longer than I might have liked – I asked him if he was still there. My faith in him was strong, but it was nice to know that he was still communicating from his perch above and behind where I was sitting.

The morning when we went up was very cold, and there was snow on the ground.

But, as we started flying, the ultraviolet rays became very potent and the MIG began to expand and heat up. I started to sweat. It was so hot that, if had I put my hand against the window, it would have been burnt. After a jolting takeoff powered by full afterburners, the MIG 25 quickly rose to six miles – the height at which passenger jets cruise. We did this sub-sonically.

Supersonic speed can only be achieved up high, because a sonic boom near the ground would break too many windows down below. As we approached the speed of sound – close to 700 miles per hour – I gazed at the instrument gauges. I knew the needles and the plane itself would jerk when we broke through the barrier.

Sure enough, just as the gauge flashed Mach 1, there was a shudder. After that, the ride became incredibly smooth. For the first time in my life, I was travelling faster than thunder. We continued to accelerate, to Mach 2, breaking the sound barrier again. There was no jolt this time, and the sensation of speed was hard to judge because there was no frame of reference. We were so far above the clouds. At 70,000 feet we reached over Mach 2, and we were still climbing. The sky had turned a very deep blue and the Earth below was distinctly curved. I could see what the 16th century Italian astronomer Galileo only guessed – the curve of the 'Big Blue Marble'. As John Gillespie Magee said in his World War Two poem *High Flight*, I had 'slipped the surly bonds of Earth … put out my hand and touched the face of God' The Earth appeared serene and unreal. Its horizon at this point was 715 miles across. We were, indeed, at the edge of the universe.

At just under 100,000 feet, travelling at almost 3,000 kilometres per hour or Mach 3, the sky was cold-black and a translucent-blue hue hung over the curvature. It was surely the most exhilarating experience imaginable, going so fast that we were covering each mile in less than two seconds. At this point, we slowed appreciably. There wasn't enough air for the jet to push against. I was now at the edge of space. Alexander and I were probably the two highest people in the world – except for the cosmonauts and astronauts on the International Space Station. Space has always held a mystical fascination for me, and that experience only heightened my enthusiasm. I'm engrossed in the mystique, the darkness and, naturally enough, I'm intrigued by the perils and the danger. I've always felt the need to explore, to satisfy my natural inquisitiveness.

Yuri Gagarin, the first man in space, was *the* hero in our house. I grew up listening to my father talk about Yuri, and how he piloted Vostok One into orbit back in 1961. The connection my father had with Yuri was that both of them grew up in poor circumstances in small villages. Yuri Gagarin was born in the village of Klushino, near Gzhatsk, the son of peasant farmers. My father was born in Hora, a small poor village in Greece.

My father considered himself to be a socialist, but I reckon he was a fair dinkum communist. He was a 'red' man, for sure. How else would you describe someone who arrives in his new country carrying a bouzouki in one arm, a shabby suitcase in the other, and a little red book with the communist manifesto of Chairman Mao in one pocket. Dad used to recall how Yuri whistled the tune 'The motherland hears, the motherland knows where her son flies in the sky' during his Vostok 1 flight.

When Gagarin won the space race for Russia – beating America's Alan Shepherd by just a few weeks – he upped the stakes in the propaganda war between the communists and the western world. In response to this action, on May 25th, 1961 President Kennedy made that famous assertion to a joint sitting of the United States Congress: 'I feel that this nation should commit itself to achieving the goal, before this decade is out, of landing a man on the moon and returning him safely to Earth'.

The Americans fulfilled JFK's commitment in 1969, but Yuri, a 'red' had become the first human to rocket into orbit. When you reflect on where the Russians came from in the years after the Second World War, they certainly staged an amazing recovery. Less than two decades earlier, they had been staring at annihilation at the hands of the Nazis and suffered over twenty million casualties. Yet here they were – 'Reds in Space' – sending up satellites and probes, and leading the race for the new space frontier.

The 1960s were a tumultuous period in world history – the Cuban missile crisis plus the assassinations of President Kennedy, his brother the US attorney general Robert Kennedy and the human rights crusader Martin Luther King. And then there was the Vietnam War, and the ignominy of a conflict that the Americans came to realise they could never win. It was the triumph of the moon landing that virtually rescued the decade for the US. The Apollo 11 mission in July 1969 fired the imagination of the world, and saved the face of America's propagandists. But once Neil Armstrong's crew had returned to Earth and the celebrations were over, the question became loud: *why are we spending all this money on putting men in space*?

The Cold War had fired the space race. Once relations thawed, the politicians lost interest in discovering the new frontier. Like so many kids, I always wanted to be an astronaut, inspired by the Apollo lunar missions – I dreamed of being Neil Armstrong, Buzz Aldrin or Yuri Gagarin. I can remember my earliest fantasies – back when I was a four year-old in Melbourne, proclaiming to the world that I wanted to become an astronaut. Unfortunately, my father delivered the cold, hard truth about why I'd never be an astronaut in my early years. He knocked me back on to terra firma. It was a crushing blow.

Fast forward to the year 2001, and imagine how I felt when I saw a CNN television report about an American man who had just become the world's first civilian space explorer and astronaut.

I had this flash of awakening when I watched American millionaire Dennis Tito boarding a mission to rocket to the International Space Station. If Tito could rocket into space, so would Nik Halik. Dennis Tito became a beacon of light for me. Bang! The space odyssey had come back into my life. Suddenly, my space dream was alive.

I had allowed my father's realism, however well-intended, to originally impoverish my space dream, but this was all in the past.

Seeing Dennis Tito was the catalyst that re-kindled my fire. After I viewed the CNN report, I set about finding out how Tito had been able to get aboard the Russian Soyuz spacecraft. Dennis Tito was a stock market investor and had accrued most of his millions through hedge funds. I too had been generating a healthy cash flow from the stock market and my property investments. I had only just retired from the music industry years prior, freeing myself up to pursue new exploits, and felt that I was in a perfect position to model Dennis Tito. I tracked down everything I could about Dennis Anthony Tito – searched his company, spoke to people who knew him, and found out who he had approached within the Russian Space Program. Using some networking contacts, I was able to participate in some spaceflight activities at the Star City cosmonaut facility where Tito trained.

Until the collapse of the Soviet Union, the Yuri Gagarin Cosmonaut Training Centre was a secret military base. Outsiders, including NATO, didn't even know it existed. Star City is just forty-five kilometres from Moscow, but it's well hidden in the forest. It didn't show up on satellite photos taken by the American U2 spy planes during the Cold War. Only after the Iron Curtain came down did the Russians open up on its location. In 2001, Russia was suffering from a credit squeeze and required funds to service the operating costs of the International Space Station. The fee paid by Dennis Tito was the cash injection the Russians needed to keep their Space Program afloat. In 1998 there had been a terrible collapse in the value of the rouble, which had left Russia technically bankrupt. Every time they launched a mission to the International Space Station, the cost to the Russians was reportedly around $US15 million.

So, by taking along a space civilian and charging him, they could afford to keep up with the deal they had struck with the Americans to maintain and build modules for the ISS in orbit. The ideal spacecraft for civilian space travel was the Soyuz TMA rocket that the Russians launched from the Baikonur Cosmodrome in Kazakhstan. The Soyuz has three seats, but needs only two pilots. The third seat could be sold off. This presented a unique opportunity for wealthy dreamers to do what NASA, The United States National Aeronautics and Space Administration would never allow – cashed up civilians to train for and rocket into space. Tito originally approached NASA, offering to pay the American Space Program for a seat on the Space Shuttle. It was only after NASA officials scoffed at the idea that a deal was eventually brokered with the Russians.

Tito had actually been a rocket scientist at JPL, the Jet Propulsion Laboratory, in Pasadena, a NASA-affiliated company, before he made his fortune on the stock market. He has always been in awe of the Apollo program that sent mankind to the moon. He had hopes himself of becoming an astronaut. He left JPL because he was disillusioned with the direction NASA took post-Apollo. I agree with Tito's disillusionment. Over the last few decades, NASA really has lost its vision. It no longer seems to be about the dream of space exploration, and more about carrying freight to orbit and unleashing satellites. There are currently 843 satellites orbiting the earth. These days NASA's program is fundamentally the Space Shuttle, an obsolete system of space transportation. The shuttle program has many dangers associated with it. In fact, the Russians abandoned their shuttle program in the 1980s – with fuel tanks strapped to the spacecraft – it was flawed and potentially dangerous. It took the loss of fourteen astronauts in two disasters, Challenger in 1987 and Columbia in 2003, for NASA to agree. NASA announced that by 2010, it will retire its space shuttle fleet.

In those grandiose years of the 1960s, NASA had been about human space exploration. It was not about sending payloads of satellites to lower orbit, like a glorified freight company. NASA used to stand for dreams. As a space enthusiast, I was intrigued by the human and engineering achievements of launching into space.

I grew up in awe of the NASA Apollo Space Program that sent man to the moon. The most vivid image I remember is the picture of Buzz Aldrin with Earth behind him and the reflection of Neil Armstrong in his visor.

Alas, the impetus for the American space program started to fade with the budget cuts of 1972 and the scrapping of the Apollo missions. Cutting back was the wrong decision, one that betrayed the space community, just when they were all set to explore other civilisations. If they had kept the space mission going, by now the question of whether other civilisations exist might well have been answered.

Frankly, I'm sure there is other life out there. Earth is just one star amongst billions of stars in the galaxy. We're not the only life form. My frustration with NASA's cutbacks is that they achieved so much in the 1960s. If they had proceeded, mankind would have reached Mars by now. The conquest of a new planetary system would have opened up yet another frontier. It could have determined whether some form of life does really exist on Mars. After all, Mars does have frozen ice caps and lots of other similarities to Earth. The past three US presidents – George Bush senior, Bill Clinton and George Bush junior – have all spearheaded Mars initiatives which have failed. Those Mars initiatives were token offerings, election-orientated, with slogans aimed at capturing the popular vote. The US has now cut back to only sending probes to Mars. NASA's focus these days is on the International Space Station.

Since the Cold War ended, the United States has primarily financed the Space Station program, running it in agreement with the Russian program. Before the US agreed to the deal to jointly run the Space Station, they demanded that the Russians abandon and de-orbit their own space station, the MIR, in favour of the International Space Station. They didn't want another competing space station in earth orbit.

After Dennis Tito's history-making trip to the ISS in 2001, I flew to Russia to visit the cosmonaut training facilities in Star City, Russia. It was tucked away in the national forest, hidden behind huge evergreen trees. On a concrete block nearing the entrance to Star City was an old MIG 21. This had always been one of my favourite jets. As I strolled through the corridors of the administration building, I thought wow, if only my father were alive to see this. The pictures on the walls were all of Soviet heroes. There were no American space conquests, and in particular, no mentioning of the first moon landing by the US. There was the first Czechoslovakian in space, the first Bulgarian in space, the first East German and Cuban in space and, of course, the first Russian and human in space, Yuri Gagarin.

I asked if they would take me to see Yuri Gagarin's old office, which had been converted into a small museum, such is his hero status. It was such a thrill for me to sit at his desk and to view the work he had been doing at the time of his death in 1968.

As I walked around the corridors and across the grounds, I thought how shabby the buildings looked. They were cold and sterile, like an old hospital. The corridors were dingy and many rooms were dark, with light bulbs missing. But the training program is still considered to be the world's best and safest. Their training facilities are legendary and their Soyuz spacecraft are incredibly robust. During my Star City visit and subsequent training, I was escorted around by Russian minders. Everyone was in uniforms, wearing lots of military brass. There were pictures of MIGs everywhere, and it's obvious the MIG holds a special place in the aviation and space history of Russia. The jets they use today still have the red star on their livery – cold war machinery that is still relevant into the 21st century. The MIGs were designed to intercept American CIA spy planes travelling at high altitudes, predominantly the U2 planes and the SR71 Blackbirds. In order to combat American spy missions, the Russians made sure the MIG 25s could fly higher and faster than any other aircraft. The chief CIA long-range supersonic reconnaissance aircraft was the SR71 Blackbird, which had an operational ceiling of 90,000 feet. The altitude level of a modified MIG 25 is around 125,000 feet. During the same week as my edge of space flight, I had my zero gravity training flight in an Ilyushin 76 experimental craft, in which we simulated weightlessness while performing various mid-air experiments. The Ilyushin 76 does this by launching into a vertical climb, then swooping into a dive, which creates the weightless environment. You've got thirty seconds of simulated weightlessness in which to perform exercises. The Americans call this experience, the 'vomit comet', because most astronauts who become initiated within a zero gravity climate are likely to throw up. In my zero gravity experience I came close, but some of the other guys lost their breakfast. I had taken a high dose of Dramamine earlier in the morning as a precaution and this assisted me to control any potential motion sickness. It was odd – and rather disquieting – to see vomit floating around in mid-air.

When I travelled to Star City in 2003, Dennis Tito and South African Mark Shuttleworth were the only civilian space explorers who had rocketed up to the International Space Station for a ten day stay, courtesy of a deal brokered by Eric Anderson from Space Adventures. Gregory Olsen followed them in 2005. Later came Anousheh Ansari and in 2007, Microsoft billionaire software engineer Charles Simonyi who helped develop two of the world's most popular software applications, Microsoft Corp's Word and Excel, paid $US25 million for the privilege of going up to the ISS. Back in 2001, Dennis paid around $US20 million for the trip that made him a worldwide celebrity. It was interesting to note that all these individuals had generated the bulk of their wealth in the stock market. Anousheh Ansari, using her savings and corporate retirement accounts, co-founded Telecom Technologies, just as a wave of deregulation hit the telecommunications industry in the US. The company was later acquired by Sonus Networks, Inc. in 2000 for $550 million in stock. Anousheh, a genuine space enthusiast, became the first female Muslim and first Iranian in space. I had the privilege of meeting her at Edwards Air Force Base in 2004 when she put up $US10 million dollars for the X Prize, a competition to launch the first privately funded space mission. The Ansari X Prize was created for the public sector to develop and fly a spacecraft into orbit and bring it back to earth. It was a great way to 'stick it up' NASA.

I was invited to Edwards Air Force Base, by Eric Anderson who paved the way for all the civilian space explorers who followed after Tito's historic orbital flight. Edwards Air Force Base was a United States Air Force base located on the border of Kern County in the Antelope Valley. Notable occurrences at Edwards Air force Base include Chuck Yeager's famous flight where he broke the sound barrier In the Bell X-1 in 1947. Eric knows that I am wildly excited about journeying deeper into space, and has been grooming me for future flights. We regularly keep in contact and have discussed space business ventures together.

The spirit of the X Prize Foundation was to stimulate interest among the civil sector in space. It was based on the Ortega prize, which was announced to stimulate flying back in the time of Charles Lindbergh and the Spirit of St Louis. The prize back then was $US10,000. The X Prize – with $US10 million offered by Anousheh Ansari – was in the spirit of the Ortega prize. During the X Prize competition, I was fortunate to meet Charles Lindbergh's grandson, Erik, who is a trustee and vice-president of the X Prize Foundation. The success of the X Prize proved that the civilian sector can send a space craft to orbit. And, in essence, it proved that NASA's days as the pioneering force in regards to space were numbered.

While I was at Edwards Air Force base for the X Prize, I met many of the privateers who could well shape the future of space travel. Among them were Burt Rutan and his company, Scaled Composites, who were personally funded by Microsoft founder Paul Allan. Rutan's crew succeeded in sending the first privately built, flown and funded space craft into space, and walked away with the $US10 million. This achievement was quickly commercialised, by Virgin Galactic, an offshoot of Sir Richard Branson's Virgin Group who will be offering flights to suborbital altitudes by 2010. Sir Richard was present during the X Prize and revealed his space tourism plans to the world.

After the completion of the X Prize competition, I was asked to be interviewed via satellite link with several major news networks across the globe regarding my space training in Russia, and to attend a special party in Los Angeles. At this special party that night, I was to meet the catalyst for my renewed space enthusiasm. Eric Anderson provided me with an unsurpassed invitation. I was formally invited to Dennis Tito's house for dinner. It was a grand opportunity to thank Dennis for inspiring me. That night I flew back to Los Angeles and was escorted to several television studios to be interviewed. Upon the conclusion of my media duties in Studio City, Dennis had arranged a private driver to pick me up from the Beverly Wiltshire Hotel in Beverly Hills. I arrived at Dennis Tito's multi-million dollar opulent home in Pacific Palisades in the hills overlooking Los Angeles at 7.30 pm.

Dennis was an amazing host and paid tribute to the historic day that had taken place at Edwards Air Force Base with *Space Ship One,* the experimental space craft reaching an altitude of 370,000 feet. Tito, a man in his 60s, provided us with a private tour of his beautiful mansion. His ten-car garage was a showcase of the finest and most exotic automotives. We sat down in his lounge sipping cocktails, watching on a giant video screen, the video camera footage he took of his flight to the International Space Station in 2001. There was an amazing shot of Dennis holding the camera to his face and – in the distance over his shoulder – was planet Earth, *no borders, no divisions and no boundaries.* When he saw the shot, he had tears in his eyes. I had tears welling up in my eyes. I think we were both moved by the thought that fantasy had become reality, and that Earth really is only a small part of the picture. I remembered back to a few years earlier, when I first saw this eccentric multi-millionaire on that CNN newscast. Now, here I was, in his home, on his couch, sharing his excitement.

In early 2007, an amazing opportunity to escape the confines of low earth orbit was presented to me. Human spaceflight was about to change forever. I was specifically chosen to represent the Asia Pacific/Australasian contingent of the world to compete in a new 'Space Reality TV' event in the US to be broadcast to millions across the globe. It was rumoured to be spearheaded by non-other than Mark Burnett, the certified genius and producer of *Survivor*, Donald Trump's *The Apprentice* and Sylvester Stallone's *The Contender*. Burnett continually raises the bar each season as he changes the reality TV concept. For example, with Donald Trump's *The Apprentice* he managed to completely blow that bar away. Leaving the tropical environment of his *Survivor* series for the streets of New York City, Burnett was now focused on a space reality TV program. *Destination: Mir* was originally proposed by Burnett in 2000, but NASA put an end to it by insisting the Russian Space Agency de-orbit the Russian MIR Orbital station and allow it to break up in Earth's atmosphere.

With the International Space Station currently being assembled in outer space, a new player and space station to the world stage had arrived. With *Destination: ISS*, twenty people from around the world, including myself, would have the opportunity to take the epic journey that so many of us have dreamed of. The twenty chosen will each be millionaires, and will have a lot more than just pride at stake. Each of those chosen would be putting up $1 million of their own money. One of these twenty is going to be launched in the Soyuz Rocket and sent into space. They will then return in a Soyuz descent module, landing in the steppes of Kazakhstan. The winning contestant will spend eight days aboard the International Space Station – mankind's only outpost in space.

There are still major hurdles before the reality TV gets off the ground. Add to this the other major problem of access to space. The Soyuz Rocket which will rocket the successful candidate into space has demonstrated its ability to meet its launch windows with high reliability. However, any Soyuz flight to the International Space Station has to first meet the mission requirements of the ISS. This requires the Russians to coordinate with NASA. The reality TV show would naturally want to show the launch live, in prime time on the US east coast, which may not be possible considering the launch window requirements of flying to the space station. The production team requires a firm commitment of a launch time and date many months in advance, far earlier than the space station partners would naturally establish such dates.

One by one, the twenty contestants will be eliminated throughout the series. In the end there will be only two people left. After extensive months of secretive training, they will be taken to Kazakhstan where the launch will be telecast live. In this barren windswept land, the winner will finally be revealed to millions of viewers worldwide watching thousands of miles away. The one who is not chosen will walk away from the launch pad, and eventually return to the usual chores of everyday life, doing the shopping, collecting the mail, walking the dog, and so forth. The winner will blast off into man's greatest frontier. This space reality TV concept nevertheless remains a logistical and bureaucratic stumbling block in order for it to receive the green light.

The future of space exploration is definitely the domain of private enterprise achievers, and as a result, NASA, because of its inactivity, has surrendered the space race to the civilian sector. NASA estimates it will cost about $US5 billion to rocket to Mars. But some futurists I've spoken with say they think they'll be able to get to Mars for less than $US500 million. The biggest problem with attempting a voyage to Mars is the fuel source. The only way to develop a source is to send a probe to create the fuel five years before you send the first manned mission. By sending a probe to design and create the fuel, they can re-fuel the manned mission to get it back to earth. It will take two years to get there and three years to manufacture the fuel, utilising some of the materials that exist on the planet. Mars is so interesting because it has strong similarities to Earth. Scientists believe Mars will be able to sustain life if they can alter its atmospheric pressure. The scientists want to release greenhouse emissions on Mars, heating it up two degrees every year. These emissions would melt the polar ice caps of Mars, creating oceans and rivers. It might then be capable of supporting life. Scientists believe that within 150 years, humanity will be able to live on Mars.

All this sounds quite bizarre, but that's exploration. I'm sure someone once questioned the sanity of Columbus or Magellan or Cook. We can't be myopic about our frontiers. Why be ordinary, when you can be extraordinary! My personal goal is to walk the lunar surface of the moon. According to my sources in Moscow, the Russians would be prepared to take a civilian to the moon for a fee of $US100 million.

Certainly, several countries have moon landings on their horizon. The Japanese have declared they want to set up a moon base by 2025. The Chinese have said they want to launch their own Taikonauts on the lunar surface by 2021. NASA has said it will build a base on the moon and land a human on Mars by 2020. I personally think the Americans will want to triumph on their return manned mission to the moon by 2017. The evolution of space exploration by 2030 could incorporate the first anti-matter drive systems that could reach speeds of more than 300 million kilometres per hour and could enable us to reach habitable, Earth-like planets beyond our solar system. By 2047, the erection of the first 'Space Elevator' made out of carbon nanotubes utilising ultra-strong cables will be anchored to the Earth's surface. This elevator reaches vertically into space by gravitational forces and allows structures to place objects into orbit by scaling the cable without having to expend as much energy as a rocket. The elevator would be a smooth 100,000 kilometre ride. Welcome to our future in space.

British physicist and mathematician Stephen Hawking quoted that the human race should reach for the stars in order to survive. Hawking said, 'It is important for the human race to spread out into space for the survival of the species.' He also went on to say that, 'Life on Earth is at an ever increasing risk of being wiped out by a disaster such as sudden global warming, nuclear war, a genetically engineered virus or other dangers we haven't yet thought of, but if we can avoid killing ourselves for the next hundred years we should have settlements that can continue without support from Earth.' Hawking predicted a lunar settlement within twenty years and a Martian colony in forty years. Mankind has no option but to explore other frontiers in space. Our population is now heading to nine billion people by the middle of this century. Earth's resources are finite and a cataclysmic event is virtually assured at some point in the future.

Space is the last bastion. Exploring it is the gamble of the unknown. We really don't know what is out there. But it's an ambition that has been building up in me all my life. If I spend my last dollar getting to the moon, it'll be worth it. Upon exploring the moon by design – I doubt I would have the desire to return back to Earth. It will be the pinnacle of my life. Starting life all over again, being stripped back to basics and experiencing a new chapter of my life. Wow!

THE THRILLIONAIRE® PRINCIPLE

- Since childhood, what do you still dream about?
- What ambitions have been building up in your life?
- Do you ever fight for the realisation of your dreams?

Chapter 8

Unveiling the money matrix

Let me tell you why you're here. You're here because you know something. What you know, you can't explain. But you feel it. You've felt it your entire life – Morpheus

By understanding the concept of money and its true origins, I was never intimidated by it. I refused to live in fear of it and at all times, I was its handler and master. With these principles I maintained control and strengthened my resolve. With your permission, I would like to expose and unveil the money matrix for you.

Firstly, imagine if I were to give you two pills to swallow. One was a red pill and the other was a blue pill. Assuming you chose the blue pill and the story ends. You wake up in your bed, nothing changes and you continue believing whatever you want to believe. But what if you were fortunate to take the red pill to really see how deep the rabbit-hole of life extends to.

Accepting the red pill earlier in my life enabled me to drill deeper into life. That state of mind had been an impenetrable fortress in the past. Soon, I developed an 'Access All Areas Pass'. The red pill permitted me to traverse the rabbit-hole of exponential thinking to manifest results on a higher physical existence that were literally 'Out-of-this-World'. By exponential thinking, I am referring to the mental faculty and ability to alter my perspective on life, the boundaries as to what was really possible and the restructuring of my internal belief system. More importantly was the attitude of never accepting the world in relation to how it appeared to me. The movie: *The Matrix*, starring Keanu Reeves, had a memorable scene regarding the human potential of the mind.

Trinity: 'This is it, let me give you one piece of advice. Be honest, he knows more than you can imagine.'

They arrive at a hotel, and Trinity takes Neo to a closed door. She turns and faces him. Neo opens the door and walks in to see a dark figure staring out of the window. He turns and smiles at Neo.

Morpheus: 'At last. Welcome, Neo. As you no doubt have guessed, I am Morpheus.'

Neo: 'It's an honour to meet you.'

Morpheus: 'I imagine that right now you're feeling a bit like Alice tumbling down the rabbit hole? Hmm?'

Neo: 'You could say that.'

Morpheus: 'I can see it in your eyes. You have the look of a man who accepts what he sees, because he is expecting to wake up. Ironically, this is not far from the truth … Do you believe in fate, Neo?'

Neo: 'No.'

Morpheus: 'Why?'

Neo: 'Because I don't like the idea that I'm not in control of my own life.'

Morpheus: 'I know exactly what you mean. Let me tell you why you're here. You're here because you know something. What you know, you can't explain. But you feel it. You've felt it your entire life. That there's something wrong with the world. You don't know what it is, but it's there ... like a splinter in your mind, driving you mad. It is this feeling that has brought you to me. Do you know what I'm talking about?'

Neo: 'The Matrix?'

Morpheus: 'The Matrix is everywhere. It's all around us, even in this very room. You can see it when you look out your window or when you turn on your television. You can feel it when you go to work and when you pay your taxes. The Matrix is the world that has been pulled over your eyes, to blind you from the truth.'

Neo: 'What truth?'

Morpheus: 'That you are a slave, Neo. Like everyone else, you were born into bondage, born into a prison that you cannot smell or taste or touch. A prison … for your mind … Unfortunately, no one can be told what the Matrix is … you have to see it for yourself.'

Morpheus opens a container which holds two pills: a blue one, and a red one. He puts one in each hand, and holds them out to Neo.

Morpheus: 'This is your last chance. After this, there is no turning back … You take the blue pill, the story ends. You wake up and believe … whatever you want to believe. You take the red pill … you stay in Wonderland … and I show you just how deep the rabbit hole goes.'

Neo pauses for an instant, than reaches for the red pill. He swallows it down with a glass of water, and looks at Morpheus.

Morpheus: 'Remember … all I'm offering you is the Truth: nothing more. Follow me …'

Just like in the movie *The Matrix*, as Morpheus says, you have two choices: the red pill or the blue pill. In relation to money, I altered my relationship with it and maintained control over it. This meant I developed the fiscal confidence to never fear it and to seek further leverage to compound its earning potential.

With regards to money, mankind has been a slave, ravaged by the manipulation and deceptive concept of it. Most of the global population is fascinated with the allure of money. What is it about money that ordinary people would kill for it, sacrifice half of their life attempting to earn it and having money control the emotions of their life.

In my case, I was searching for an answer that I believed had plagued humanity for over a century. I finally discovered it.

So what really is money? What if I was to tell you that money did not actually exist. In essence, money is just a concept. There's much more digital money in circulation than money that exists in its physical form. My mental awakening to these esoteric concepts transformed my ability to have money attracted to me in my later life. By understanding how money was created, I then set out to develop the applicable cash flow strategies that would fuel my lifestyle and investments.

How did all of this get started you might ask? The concept of paper money and the lending component of it began in medieval England around 1024 AD by the early moneychangers. The moneychangers were simply goldsmiths who stored other people's gold for safekeeping in their vaults. On receipt of this gold, goldsmiths issued gold deposit receipts to the owners. This was the advent of paper money. The first 'paper' money in Western Europe was merely a receipt for gold left with the goldsmith, made from rag paper. There was a saying back then:

'Rags make paper; paper makes money; money makes banks; banks make loans; loans make beggars; beggars make rags.'

Paper money caught on because it was more convenient, and safer to carry than a lot of heavy gold and silver coins. As a convenience, to avoid unnecessary trips to the goldsmiths, depositors began endorsing these gold deposit receipts to others, using their signature.

To simplify the process, the receipts were eventually made out to the bearer making them easily transferable, without the need for an endorsing signature. This dramatic sequence of events severed the tie to any identifiable deposit of gold. Eventually, goldsmiths noticed that only a small fraction of depositors or bearers ever came in and demanded their gold at one time. Goldsmiths proceeded to cheat on the system. They began secretly lending out some of the gold that was entrusted to them for safekeeping, and kept the interest earned on the actual lending.

The goldsmiths then begun to print more gold deposit certificates than gold they had in reserve. They discovered they could lend out or fractionalise additional paper money and charge interest on it as well. This was the deceptive birth of *Fractional Reserve Lending*. Loaning out more funds than the reserves you have on deposit. This fraudulent and elaborate scam continues to this day and would be punishable by a lengthy prison term if any of us had masterminded it.

The goldsmiths began with relatively modest cheating, lending out in gold deposit certificates only two or three times the amount of gold that they actually possessed in their vaults. But they soon grew more astute and greedy, lending out four, five and up to ten times more gold certificates than they had gold on deposit.

So, for example, if $1,000 in gold were deposited with the goldsmiths, they could lend out about $10,000 in paper money and charge interest on it, and no one would discover the deceptive and brazen conduct. Goldsmiths gradually accumulated more and more wealth and used this wealth to accumulate more and more gold.

It was this abuse of trust and fraud which became accepted as standard practice. This later evolved into our modern day banking system. Today, this practice of lending out more money than there are reserves is known as Fractional Reserve Banking.

Then along came the banks. They were able to fractionalise their money, on the accounts of what people had in savings. The bank's system of manipulation is that they encourage debt, mortgages, personal loans, car loans and credit cards. The system works beautifully for those in control. If individuals live in fear of debt, then the population is much easier to sedate and control. Debt maintains the status quo and the self-perpetuating cycle. What a perfectly orchestrated scam. The education system weighs in as part of the system with its lack of fiscal education in our school curriculums to ensure ninety-five per cent of the population work by necessity and remain a few months from being dead broke. Individuals are conditioned to embrace debt and to live in hope. Effectively, the world's money system of credit has been annexed and controlled by up to 750 families. These private individuals control the system of credit in the world, the governments, the societies, the banking systems and all the financial institutions.

This paper and digital currency that bankers create out of thin air is backed by nothing. Banks loan out more money than they could ever store in their vaults. The more paper dollars that roll off the printing presses or digital dollars created by computers, the less each one is worth. Therefore, it takes more printed currency to buy the things we need, so the price of everything has to continue rising and rising. Unfortunately, wages for most people will not increase fast enough to stay ahead of the game. But not to worry, the international bankers developed plastic money by the name of 'credit cards' to be our saviour and help us out. They obviously didn't bother to tell us that they do not create enough paper or digital currency to pay off the debt plus interest so mathematically the economy will eventually collapse as has always occurred in history with paper currencies.

Banks can create this phony 'currency' out of thin air and can loan out what they don't even have. When you apply for a loan from a bank, the bank does not have anything to back up that loan. In fact if every citizen was to withdraw their money from the banks at the exact same time, the entire banking system would collapse.

Historically, financial institutions have been allowed to loan out up to thirty times more 'currency' than they have on deposit. This equates for up to thirty fictional dollars to one real dollar. They simply create 'money' out of thin air. It only costs them a few cents to print each 'dollar bill', and then they 'bill' the population for the full face value of the note. Then to add insult to injury, they charge interest on the borrowing of their so-called 'money'. If you or I were to transact this, we would be arrested for counterfeiting and fraud.

We have in this world, one of the most corrupt banking institutions responsible for this. I refer to the Federal Reserve Board and the Federal Reserve Banks. The first misconception that most people have is that the Federal Reserve Bank is a branch of the US government. This is incorrect. The Federal Reserve Bank is a privately owned company. Most people believe it is as American as the constitution. The fact is the constitution forbids its legal existence. *Article 1, Section 8 of the Constitution* states that congress shall have the power to create money and regulate the value thereof, not a myriad of international bankers! Today the Federal Reserve Bank controls monetary supply and profits by printing worthless paper, called money, through the treasury, regulating its value, and the biggest outrage of all, collecting interest on it. The Federal Reserve Bank creates money from nothing, and loans it back to us through banks, and charges interest on our currency. The Federal Reserve, at the head of the financial throne, also buys government debt with money printed on a printing press and charges taxpayers interest.

Who actually owns the Federal Reserve Central Banks? The foreign ownership of the twelve main central banks who own the Federal Reserve is listed below. A very well kept secret is finally revealed.

1. Rothschild Bank of London
2. Rothschild Bank of Berlin
3. Warburg Bank of Hamburg
4. Warburg Bank of Amsterdam
5. JP Morgan Corporation and the Rockefeller family
6. Lehman Brothers of New York
7. Lazard Brothers of Paris
8. Kuhn Loeb Bank of New York
9. Israel Moses Seif Banks of Italy
10. Goldman, Sachs of New York
11. Warburg Bank of Amsterdam
12. Chase Manhattan Bank of New York

This 'Illuminati' consortium of bankers rule and control the world through debt, which is the money they create out of nothing and charge interest on it. The Illuminati is a secret society founded in the late eighteenth century. It was established as a 'shadowy hand behind the throne' consortium to control world affairs through present day governments and to create and manipulate the 'New World Order'. They are private credit swindlers who prey upon the citizens of the globe for the benefit of themselves and their foreign customers, enslaving every citizen of the world.

The Federal Reserve Bank is the agent of the foreign central banks who control the creation of digital money. Those who controlled the money and banking system had at their complete disposal the most robust and full spectrum of power with which to control the course of the global financial markets.

The immense transfer of such concentrations of wealth and power were likely by design, engineered with full intent to preserve and perpetuate its existence. This exclusive reservation of such powers for this elite class would guarantee ultimate power for their descendants for generations to come.

There were early signs of the impending money deception even as far back as the 1800s.

'If the American people ever allow private banks to control the issue of their currency, first by inflation and then by deflation, the banks and corporations that will grow up around them will deprive the people of all property until their children wake up homeless on the continent their fathers conquered.' – Thomas Jefferson (1816)

'You are a den of vipers! I intend to rout you out, and by the Eternal God I will rout you out. If the people only understood the rank injustice of our money and banking system, there would be a revolution before morning.' – President Andrew Jackson (1829–1837)

How did it happen? On November 22nd 1910, Senator Nelson Aldrich, maternal grandfather to the Rockefellers, and representatives of a Monetary Commission met at a private hunting club of J P Morgan on Jekyll Island, Georgia. Their objective was to draft a bill that would put the economic future of the globe into the hands of a few private money powers. After previous attempts to push the Federal Reserve Act through Congress, this same group of powerful bankers funded and staffed Woodrow Wilson's campaign for president. Wilson had committed to sign this Act. The US Federal Reserve Act was railroaded through a carefully prepared Congressional Conference Committee meeting scheduled when most members were sleeping on Monday December 22nd, 1913 at the unlikely hour of 3.00 am. Senator Nelson Aldrich pushed the Federal Reserve Act through Congress just before Christmas when much of Congress was on vacation. At 6.02 pm on December 23rd, when many members had already left the capital for the Christmas holidays, President

Woodrow Wilson signed the Federal Reserve Act of 1913 into law. Republicans and other senators would later comment, they had no prior knowledge of the contents of the bill or could even recollect sighting it. The Federal Reserve Act transferred control of the money supply of the United States of America from Congress to the private banking elite.

Six years later in 1919, Woodrow Wilson remorsefully replied, referring to the Federal Reserve:

> 'I am a most unhappy man. I have unwittingly ruined my country. A great industrial nation is controlled by its system of credit. Our system of credit is concentrated. The growth of the nation, therefore, and all our activities are in the hands of a few men. We have come to be one of the worst ruled, one of the most completely controlled and dominated governments in the civilised world – no longer a government by free opinion, no longer a government by conviction and the vote of the majority, but a government by the opinion and duress of a small group of dominant men.'

Business leaders committed treason by giving these bankers the power to create money out of thin air backed only by the credit, meaning the taxes paid by the citizens. In 1913, when the Federal Reserve Act was fraudulently pushed through Congress, Congressman Charles Lindbergh said:

'When the President signs this bill; the invisible government by the Monetary Power will be legalised … The day of reckoning is only a few years removed. The new law will create inflation whenever the trust wants inflation … From now on, depression will be scientifically created.'

The Great Depression of the 1930s was not accidental. It was a carefully contrived occurrence by contracting the amount of currency in circulation by one third from 1929 to 1933. The international bankers conspired to bring about a condition of despair in the world so that they would emerge as rulers of us all. This is an era of economic misery for which the Federal Reserve Board and banks are fully liable.

From the Great Depression in the 1930s, the major recession in the 1990s to the bursting of the dotcom bubble in 2001, every economic downturn suffered in the world over the last eighty years can be traced to the Federal Reserve policy. Millions across the globe became unemployed. As a result of the financial calamity and manipulated economic downturn of the global Great Depression in the 1930s, six of my father's older siblings perished. The Federal Reserve has followed a consistent policy of flooding the global economy with easy money, leading to an artificial 'boom' followed by a recession or depression when the Federal Reserve induced bubble bursts.

The movie, *The Matrix* echo's the choice of the influential and affluent who prefer the virtual reality shown by the mass media to the true reality of human suffering and evil. As a society, we should be reprogrammed to re-establish rapport with our conscious mind and raise our level of awareness. By dismantling the boundary condition of thoughts, we empower ourselves to eradicate the tyranny of conditioned thinking. We therefore simply need to make a conscious decision to take the red pill, unplug ourselves from the System, set our minds free, open the door, walk through the door, keep it open and propel ourselves towards our divine destiny.

THE THRILLIONAIRE® PRINCIPLE

- Have you enabled yourself to drill deeper into life by accepting the 'Red Pill'?
- Do you believe in fate?
- Have you dismantled the tyranny of conditioned thinking?

Chapter 9

Seven Summits quest

Why seek to scale Mount Everest, Queen of the Air,
Why strive to crown that cruel crest and deathward dare?
Said Mallory of dauntless quest …
'Because it's there.'
– George Leigh Mallory as quoted in *Dauntless Quest* by Robert Service

The intrepid British mountaineer George Mallory was on a lecture tour in America in 1923 when a reporter from the *New York Times* asked him why he wanted to climb Mt Everest. After persistent questioning, Mallory gave a three word response: '*Because it's there*'. The quote became one of the most famous in history, not least because Mallory lost his life on Everest in the following year. The George Mallory story fascinates me. Hearing about the English schoolmaster's attempts to climb Everest got me interested in mountain climbing. Sometimes it's the hard luck stories, the tragedies and the controversies that occupy our thinking more than the conquests.

Mallory is part of the aura of Mt Everest. He gave his life for that mountain.

Climbing Everest is a dream for so many people, one they consider to be worth risking everything to fulfil. Why? Because it's still there.

When I viewed a documentary on the ill-fated Everest expedition of 1924, I thought Mallory was a real storybook hero. The speculation about whether he might well have climbed Everest almost a quarter of a century before Edmund Hillary and Tenzing Norgay only added to the intrigue. History acknowledges New Zealand beekeeper Hillary and Sherpa Tenzing as the first to conquer the world's highest peak in 1953.

But the 1999 expedition that found the remains of George Mallory raised some questions about who really was the first, and whether Mallory and his climbing partner Andrew Irvine made it in 1924. Mallory's body was found at 27,000 feet, two thousand feet short of the summit. The analysis work done on his frozen remains and the angle of his body suggests he may have fallen two or three thousand feet down the north-east face. He had fallen from near the summit – or, quite possibly, from the summit itself. So, after that discovery in May 1999, the question was asked, 'Were George and Andrew Irvine the first to summit Everest?'

I have heard many arguments regarding the Mallory summit mystery. Some believe that an assault on Everest is only successful if you live to tell the tale. Maybe so, but George Mallory's achievement was inspirational. The schoolmaster perished on his third attempt on the mountain. A sad demise, but what an adventurer he was. Mt Everest isn't just the highest place on the planet. Its name is a synonym for anything that is the biggest, hardest or toughest.

The ultimate challenge, in any form of endeavour, is the 'Everest'. What makes people want to push themselves past their limit – and go further than anyone considered possible – is a will to extend their boundaries. Within us, there is a need to test ourselves beyond where we have gone – to reach our zenith. There is no greater conquest then to set foot on the peak of Everest, the rooftop of Earth – all 29,028 feet or 8,847 metres of it. The mountains are silent teachers and enlighten the path to noble qualities: humility towards nature, sacrifice and willpower.

It is my ambition to climb Everest in the coming months. I've been building and preparing myself for this mission, one way or another, since I was a schoolboy. Before I tackle Everest, however, I am in the process of accomplishing the other famed summits of the world. Only about twenty per cent of those who do attempt Everest reach the summit and the mountain claims the lives of climbers every season. Even the most experienced mountaineers face life-threatening situations on Everest. The weather can turn in minutes, stranding climbers at high altitudes in subzero temperatures or triggering an avalanche that can bury an entire team in an instant. Even under optimal conditions, one misstep can lead to a fatal fall.

I have a lot of respect for the mountain. Over the past few years I have climbed the highest peaks of four continents, including the mighty Mt Aconcagua in the Andes. I have three more peaks to summit to become one of 200 climbers in history who have climbed the Seven Summits – the highest mountains of all seven of the world's continents. My last climb of the seven will be the *big kahuna* itself, the high priest of all mountains – Mt Everest. Of course George Mallory was simplifying things a little when he offered, 'because it's there'. No doubt George had thought long and hard about what he wanted to achieve. Sometimes though, trying to explain your motivation to someone who doesn't understand is as difficult as climbing the mountain itself.

I believe everyone who sets their sights on such a momentous mission gives plenty of thought to why they want to do it. We all have the identifiable 'why' reasoning which manifests the paths we pursue in life. Before I embark on any adventure that I tackle, I always research my 'why' factor. When you know something will alter you physically, emotionally and spiritually, you need a strong 'why' factor in order to fulfil your destiny. You need an emphatic reasoning to your 'why' factor in order for it to motivate you, especially when it is so easy to find a thousand reasons to retreat and turn back.

The quote by Harold V Melchert best validated my love for mountaineering.

'Live your life each day as you would climb a mountain. An occasional glance toward the summit keeps the goal in mind, but many beautiful scenes are to be observed from each new vantage point. Climb slowly, steadily, enjoying each passing moment; and the view from the summit will serve as a fitting climax for the journey.'

I feel it's important to write my goals down. When I embrace new ideas at any stage during the day, I relay them onto a voice recorder immediately. I then transcribe and write the ideas down. Spoken words too easily evaporate.

Written words leave impressions. I wrote my lifetime goals a long time ago, back when I was still in primary school. This was the initial fertilising of the seed that had the potential to manifest infinite greatness. I still adhere to those goals and – over the years – I have lived and breathed them. When you think about something long enough, and visualise it repeatedly, you begin to believe you can achieve it.

Anything the mind can conceive and believe it can achieve. A belief system is mandatory. If you don't believe you can do something, you'll make up any excuse to remove yourself from achieving it. I call that 'excusitis', the failure disease which leads to procrastination which fertilises more fear.

With my plans and preparations to summit Mt Everest, I have spoken with several people who have climbed it. I've listened in great detail to Everest survivors who made the summit of Everest, as well as others who I believe have a realistic knowledge of what's involved. On the *Titanic* dive in 2005, I met Eric O'Connor, an American adventure and thrill-seeker who successfully summited Everest just a couple of months earlier. Eric was the son of Sandra Day O'Connor, the first woman to be appointed as a US Supreme Court Justice. The yarns he told on board the mother ship *Akademik Keldysh*, en route to *Titanic*, were riveting. Quite possibly he embellished them a little, but Eric sure knows how to get the most out of life. A week before the *Titanic* expedition, Eric and his entourage chartered a plane over the Arctic and parachuted over the North Pole. They had a bet on who could land their parachute closest to 90 degrees north. Eric told me that on his Everest summit push, his oxygen bottle froze on a forty-foot vertical climb, known as the Hillary Step. When he finally made it to the Everest summit and to further exacerbate the crisis, his cornea suffered a high degree of frostbite. It must have been incredibly cold, and he was lucky to survive. Fortunately, he had acclimatised well, and he was still able to breathe enough to get through the crisis.

The summit of Everest, the highest point in the world is covered with assorted prayer flags, offerings, mementos and discarded oxygen bottles. The panoramic view unveils the Tibetan plateau to the north, and the great Himalayan peaks of Kanchenjunga to the east, Makalu to the south-east, and Cho Oyu to the west.

Everest is plagued with a myriad of challenges, including the infamous Khumbu Icefall. The icefall is located at the head of the Khumbu Glacier, just above Base Camp, and is one of the most treacherous parts of an ascent from the South Col of Nepal. The movement of the glacier can cause large crevasses to open, with little warning, or can hide crevasses buried under snow. Large towers of ice, ranging in size from a car to a large house can collapse suddenly. The continually shifting nature of the icefall makes crossing it very dangerous. Next you have the 'Death Zone'. This term refers to any altitude above 26,250 feet where the amount of oxygen cannot sustain human life. The body cannot acclimatise, and staying longer than necessary results in the deterioration of bodily functions, loss of consciousness, and inevitable death. The last real challenge before ascending the summit is the Hillary Step. It is a nearly vertical, forty-foot outcropping of snow and ice at about 28,750 feet. At the Hillary Step, there's a 28,750 foot drop – to Tibet on one side, and Nepal on the other. To negotiate this formidable step in your oxygen-starved brain will push you to the extreme limits of human survival.

After months of preparation, climbers can spend no more than twenty minutes on the summit, as they need to descend to the South Col before midday. Darkness sets in during the afternoon and weather changes are sudden, and can easily trap climbers. Eric told me the challenge of Everest was everything he expected. He reiterated that it is one of the biggest challenges any person can commit their mind and body to. The dangers only served to heighten my enthusiasm about this Himalayan monolith. I'm attracted to danger. Listening to Eric, I could sense the romance, the heightened feeling of awareness that you feel when you're on the edge. It's spine-tingling. I enjoy being on the razor's edge, and there is no sharper ridge than at the highest spot on the planet.

I've studied so much about Everest. I've visualised the terrain, the Khumbu Icefall, the base camps up to South Col, the Hillary step, the Cornice Traverse, right to the final staging post before climbers make their final push to the summit. In a book titled *Mountain without Mercy* by celebrated American climber Ed Viesturs, he said 'You don't assault Everest. You sneak up on it, and then get the hell outta there.'

Few people get the opportunity to tackle Everest. For starters, time is paramount.

There is a short climbing season – just the month of May. For the rest of the year, the winds and snowfalls are so suicidal that climbing is well-nigh impossible. Anyone attempting to summit Everest must be able to commit three to four months in the Himalayas beforehand to acclimatise themselves. This is critical, as climbing rotations up and down to higher elevations helps the body to develop red blood cells and become acclimatised to the higher altitude. If you don't acclimatise, you don't stand a chance. They say that if you stepped from a helicopter onto the Everest summit, you'd be dead within fifteen minutes.

Climbing at extreme high altitude ravages the human body. Most climbers, even the fittest, could lose fifteen to twenty kilograms in the attempt. At 26,000 feet your body is effectively dying. You're not eating, not sleeping and not getting enough oxygen to the brain. Up there, you're in what is so aptly called the Death Zone. Consequently, only the most committed individuals are prepared to put themselves through it. There's another commitment – the investment required. It costs each climber between $US60,000 and $US80,000 to be part of an Everest expedition. It's no small consideration, especially when it's in addition to all the other sacrifices people have to make to get there. The cost of joining expeditions makes Everest a fairly selfish mountain quest. Because expedition members have already sacrificed so much in time and money, they don't want to abandon their attempts. They'll stretch boundaries to keep their hopes alive.

The biggest controversy on Everest at the moment is that climbing has become too commercialised. Unless you have the funds, you can't even think about it. And some of those who do have the unlimited monetary supply have been accused of not caring enough for the Himalayan environment or their Sherpa guides. The Sherpas are an ethnic group from the most mountainous region of Nepal, high in the Himalaya. Edmund Hillary and other veterans are saying that there should be a moratorium on all Everest climbing, and that the mountain should be given time to heal. I doubt that will ever happen.

Climbers are a significant source of tourist revenue for Nepal. The Nepalese government requires a permit from all prospective climbers, which carries a heavy fee, often more than $US25,000 per person. The Sherpas are far too reliant on the climbing fees that sustain their livelihood.

Everest is a bizarre place, with 203 souls having lost their lives already on this goddess mother of the snows. It is littered with over 160 bodies. The conditions on the mountain are so difficult that the corpses have been left where they fell. Some corpses are easily visible from the standard climbing routes and are a constant reminder of the peril faced. Any attempt to bring a dead climber back down the mountain is usually laden with further danger. Before climbers tackle the mountain, they are given a form to complete, in the event of their untimely death and asked to tick a box – whether they'd prefer to be shoved into a crevasse, or be left on the higher peaks forever. Personally, I'd rather choose the latter.

It's because of the 'Death Zone' – and my need to build up to the biggest challenge of all – that I'm leaving Everest as the last peak in my climbing quest on the world's Seven Summits. Everest will be the ultimate pinnacle, with new vantage and observation points. My philosophy on climbing – and the challenges of life, for that matter – is that it all comes down to how determined you are about wanting to conquer them.

When I climb a peak, what I had previously viewed as my highest vantage point changes to the polar opposite to become a support level. I then seek a new vantage point for the next peak. That's why I climb. Besides the reward of reaching my goal, I've always loved the outdoors, and I enjoy the process of climbing. Over the past two decades I have scaled many small peaks, around 5,000 feet, mainly in Australia and Europe. I love the views, the mountain air, the freshness and cold breeze in my face. I must admit I'm a Mediterranean person by nature. I'm not genetically designed for winter, but I love the mountains. The dangers are intoxicating. I know each climb will demand every ounce of my spirit to establish my new vantage point on the summit. After tackling small peaks for many years, in 2004 I advanced to higher, tougher peaks.

Kristo Panos, a close relation who lives in the San Bernardino region of Southern California has a 10,560 foot peak, named Mt Baldy, virtually at his back door. In 2004 we decided to climb it together. The cardinal rule of mountaineering is to have a climbing partner you can trust. You must have a climbing buddy. Kristo originates from the Spartan region of Southern Greece, which is famous for the extraordinary warrior-athletes who battled the invading Persian Empire during the Battle of Thermopylae in 480 BC. Kristo is tough, durable and tenacious. When you're banking on someone, depending on each other, you need to have someone whose ability you can rely on. When we started climbing higher peaks together we were embarking on a very sharp learning curve. In August 2004, Kristo and I were sitting by the poolside of his parent's home and I asked the obvious question, 'Kristo, have you ever climbed Mt Baldy?' He said he'd always wanted to, so we quickly made plans to summit it. I am an incredibly impatient individual, so I insisted we climb it the very same day. These were the early climbing days, and I certainly wouldn't recommend this approach to anyone starting out. We were way too impetuous.

Climbers who tackle Mt Baldy must report to the ranger station so that the authorities can track your movements on the mountain. California at the time was experiencing a heatwave and scorching temperatures were the cause of many heat-related deaths. The ranger informed us that we couldn't have picked a worse time in the year. August is the height of summer in the United States with temperatures well above 37 °C or 98 °F. He warned us there were abundant rattlesnakes on the climbing trek. 'Do you also know that there are grizzly bears up there, and that it's bear season?' he asked. 'Do you have water?' he enquired. In truth, all we had were two cans of Red Bull, two bananas and a muesli bar. We just wanted to climb that mountain – even though we were so under-prepared. Anyhow, we did summit the peak of Mt Baldy and we were fortunate not to encounter any grizzlies or rattlesnakes. When we returned to Kristo's house late in the evening, I shared with him that I had long held a burning desire to climb the Seven Summits of the world. There and then, we vowed to summit all seven together.

To get myself into perfect physical condition for climbing, I increased my dedication to working out. I'm generally fit – my diet is generally Mediterranean and I keep in good shape. But mountaineering requires a very fit mind and body, one that can make smart decisions in real adversity, so I bulked up with cardio-vascular work, pumped weights in the gym, and worked hard on my leg strength. I've learnt that a lot of mountaineering is done above the shoulders – it's mental. However, I also get a real buzz out of the physical aspect of climbing. When you are walking or climbing in the mountains, you're on your feet for ten to fourteen hours a day. And, while your body is under duress, your mind has plenty of time to aerate and think.

I find that my most inspiring ideas arise when I'm climbing. I thrive on the combination of putting my mind under pressure and then letting it run free. It's a real contrast. That's also how I work – I go hard at investing for eight months of each year, and then I do something completely detached for the other four months.

Time out is my time to re-charge. That is when I re-assess and re-define myself. When I'm walking or climbing, I'm continually brainstorming. I record my ideas onto a voice recorder. Wherever I go, I always carry a digital voice recorder to download any information onto my laptop. Naturally, the laptop travels everywhere with me. I think about the business and I mull over the targets I'd like to achieve, whether they are professional or personal. I visualise ways to refine my businesses, refining systems, investment strategies, methods that will ensure I'm in a perpetual state of peak performance.

In March 2005, Kristo and I summited Mt Kilimanjaro, in Tanzania, the rooftop of the continent of Africa. Kilimanjaro, rising to 19,340 feet is a Masai word meaning 'large rock'. It is the world's highest free-standing mountain and one of the world's largest volcanos. With the warming of the planet, Mt Kilimanjaro is drawing vast global attention. The mountain peak has seen a retreat of the most recent covering of glaciers, with the ice cap volume dropping by more than eighty per cent. Ice core specialists have predicted that ice on top of Mt Kilimanjaro will be gone by 2015. Interestingly enough, the summit of Kilimanjaro is covered by a GSM mobile phone network, provided by Vodacom. It lost its claim as the highest point in the world with mobile phone service, as China Mobile now provides coverage at the top of Mt Everest. As with each summit conquest came the recuperation period to heal the mind and body. With the success of the Mt Kilimanjaro climb, we made reservations to stay at the Burj Al Arab, a seven-star hotel in Dubai. Designed to resemble a billowing sail, the building soars to a height of 321 metres, dominating the Dubai coastline. At night, it offers an unforgettable sight, surrounded by choreographed colour sculptures of water and fire.

Our next successful summit was Mt Elbrus. Mt Elbrus, standing at 18,510 feet is a strato-volcano that has been dormant for about 2000 years and is considered to be the rooftop of Europe. Elbrus is in the Caucasus region, sandwiched between Dagestan and Chechnya, in a strife-torn part of Russia.

Our next big challenge was Cerro Aconcagua in Argentina, the highest peak of the Americas and highest in the western and southern hemispheres. It is the second highest of the famous Seven Summits and the amount of oxygen on the summit is comparable to an 8,000 metre peak in the Himalayas. About 500 climbers attempt Aconcagua every December to January. We made plans to summit the highest point in the Andes mountain range on Christmas Day 2006.

Climbers will tell you that – in many ways – Aconcagua is as tough as Everest, mainly because of the extreme weather patterns, particularly the notorious 'Viento Blanco' or 'white wind', a white cloud shaped like a mushroom. The Viento Blanco has a fury all of its own. It can reach speeds over 200 kilometres per hour, and climbers have been literally blown off the mountain. Every year, Mt Aconcagua claims the lives of quite a few climbers. There's a lot of history and mythology about Aconcagua. Kristo and I were determined to summit this pinnacle of the Andes. From Buenos Aires we caught a plane to the town of Mendoza, which is on the border of Chile, the starting point for any Aconcagua expedition. Mendoza is a remote agricultural town surrounded by pristine mountains. The valley is one of the great wine-growing areas of Argentina, picturesque and pastoral. Kristo and I hooked up with an adventure company based in Mendoza, where we joined up with a mini-United Nations of adventurers – among them climbers from the Netherlands, Czech Republic, Australia, United States, England and Germany. All nine in the expedition party were in harmony about their goal – to reach the summit of Cerro Aconcagua at 22,841 feet. We left the first staging post at Puente Del Incas on December 14th, planning to make the summit on the eleventh day.

After five days of trekking, on December 19th, we made it to the Plaza de Mulas base camp at 14,340 feet. This is a landmark for every expedition. For many, it is as far as they go. Every climber who tackles Aconcagua must at this point undergo a medical examination. The rules are strictly adhered to. Within two hours of making base camp at 14,340 feet, climbers have to register and see one of the medics. The check-up is to test if the climber has acclimatised and has enough available oxygen to continue the journey. If the adventurer's body hasn't acclimatised enough to produce red blood cells, the availability of oxygen will be low. It's the body's ability to produce red blood cells at a rapid rate that enables climbers to go higher. As the air thins, however, everyone becomes short of breath. The air is so thin further on up the mountain that the authorities won't allow climbers with insufficient oxygen-generating capacity to put themselves and their climbing parties at risk. Pulse oximetry measuring tests are conducted and the percentage of haemoglobin saturated with oxygen is calculated. This oxygen saturation is a measure of how much oxygen the blood is carrying as a percentage of the maximum it could carry.

To be allowed to proceed and climb at a higher altitude, all mountaineers must have a pulse oximetry measurement higher than eighty. Three members of our climbing party had counts below seventy. Because they failed their test, they were sent back down the mountain. It's an inglorious failure – you either go back by mule, or serious cases are taken down to Mendoza by helicopter. Two of the three men in our party had early signs of pulmonary oedema, otherwise known as fluid in the lungs, or acute mountain sickness. Fortunately, my score on the oximeter was eighty-eight, one of the highest in our group, and rather pleasing for a lad who was told by doctors that his asthma would hold him back in life.

We observed many climbers turning back at Plaza de Mulas, and we met others who had climbed further up the mountain only to give up and turn around. Of roughly 500 who tackle Aconcagua every summer, only about ninety actually make it to the summit. As we trekked up, meeting other parties coming back down, we asked them if they had been to the summit. So often, we were greeted by looks of despair. The taste of disappointment is bitter, especially when so much planning and preparation goes into each expedition. Most climbers told stories of the gruesome weather they'd encountered, and how they hadn't expected the conditions to be so utterly brutal.

We met one group of climbers who had all conquered Everest, and yet had come up short on Aconcagua. For one tired mountaineer, this had been his third attempt. For other climbers, Aconcagua was their Everest practice run. We were well-warned that this was a bad season for weather in the Andes.

At those heights, there are so many variables that determine your success or failure.

The biggest question is whether the mountain will 'give you permission' to climb it.

The air is so bitterly cold. The winds are relentless. Your body starts to degenerate and slowly decay. You lose your appetite. You suffer dehydration so badly you're forced to drink about eight litres of water to hydrate your system against the dryness, and yet you urinate seven litres a day. On Aconcagua, only the weather gods know what the white wind will do. When we reached 19,360 feet, at an advanced base camp called Berlin, a blizzard swept across the mountain, and all we could do was to pitch our tents and ensure we did not freeze. Berlin is nothing more than a crop of rocky terrain off the back of a glacier. There are no comforts. We pitched our tents next to a glacier. The winds roared at well over 100 kilometres per hour, the temperatures were merciless at –27 °C or –16 °F, and an ice storm raged around us. The cold was so painful that we couldn't leave our two-man tents. We peed into bottles, because it was too cold to go outside. Kristo and I drew straws as to who would have to go out to collect ice and snow to melt on our stove for water. The ice storm raged on for two days, then three, then four.

As it carried on into its fifth day, jeopardising our chances of going any further, there was nothing we could do but wait. We maintained our vigilance in our tents, reading books, planning the next mountain climb in Alaska, anything to take our minds off the chill. It was too cold to do anything; too cold to sleep. We slept for maybe an hour a night, and woke up shivering. The ice seemed to spear through the zipper of our tent. Using my satellite phone, I telephoned my mother back in Melbourne on Christmas Day. She told me it was a beautiful day in Melbourne and – like any mother would – she asked me if I was eating well and taking care of myself. I told her (through chattering teeth) that the trip was going fine and that I had more than enough to eat. If she only knew!

As cold as it was, getting stuck for days on end, near the rooftop of the Andes, was an amazing experience. It was an awakening. We really were on life's edge. Altitude does weird things to the brain. Because there's less oxygen, your thinking slows down. Simple tasks like tying a shoelace become difficult. The mental state is critical. Most deaths on the world's great mountains occur when climbers are on the descent phase of a climb. They've used everything in the tank in the climb to get to the top, and they haven't saved enough to come back down. It's a struggle to bring yourself down safely, let alone help anyone else who might be in difficulty.

Our original plan of spending Christmas Day on the summit had to be revised.

Because we were stranded for five days in Berlin advanced base camp, we had used up all the contingency days we had for our expedition. If the weather didn't ease on the sixth day, our buffer would diminish and we would be forced to retreat. Anconcagua would reign supreme over us.

Amazingly, on our sixth day at Berlin, the wind stopped briefly, and the sun peered out from between the snow white clouds. It was as if the mountaintop said to us, 'Hey, come up and see me.' It felt to me like an omen. I remember thinking about the pilot whales that escorted us in the early part of the dive down to *Titanic*, and how maybe this time it was the gods of the Andes communicating to us. Because we had used up our buffer, we had to seize our opportunity to make it to the top. The last push for the summit, at 22,841 feet, became an eighteen-hour trek. We left at 5 am, powering up the mountain, determined not to let anything hold us back. The upper part of the summit was clearly visible by now. Our next major hurdle was the feared Canaleta at 21,326 feet. As we hiked up this fifty-five degree, long gully, the final push to the summit had become almost unbearable. The Canaleta became steeper and steeper as we progressed to the final 200-foot region of the summit. The teamwork involved was incredible and the satisfaction of making the top, on the afternoon of December 29th was, to say the least, extraordinary.

Cerro Aconcagua, the stone sentinel at 22,841 feet, or 6,962 metres, was conquered! Hasta la Victoria Siempre!

Besides the six climbers who made it, we had a little *runaway* who tagged along us for that climb. A Labrador dog followed us all the way from base camp to the summit.

Our Argentine guides named him Moucho, and he had obviously done the trek several times. When we were snowed in, he seemed to find a hiding place somewhere. I have no idea where he slept during the blizzard. But when we made the eighteen-hour dash for the summit, he came with us. He was quite some climber, Moucho. The conquest of Cerro Aconcagua meant that I had climbed four of the Seven Summits. That's four down with three peaks remaining.

As we descended, I had a crazy thought. It was New Year's Eve tomorrow night and I mentioned to Kristo that we should charter a helicopter to fly us off the mountain. That way we could get back to our hotel in Mendoza to rest, heal and have a major New Year's Eve celebration. Otherwise we would not make it back to Mendoza until the third of January. Problem was, we were still at an altitude that was too dangerous for a helicopter pickup. The lift developed by a helicopter's rotors depends on the density of air. The higher the altitude, the less dense the air and so helicopters have a strict operational ceiling which prevents them from climbing any higher. After lengthy satellite phone discussions with park rangers and a helicopter charter service, we were instructed to climb down to an altitude below 15,000 feet in order to carry out the airlift. We were definitely at the ceiling of a helicopter's ability at this altitude. On December 30th, at 11.45 in the morning, after an anxious and lengthy wait, we were finally greeted by our Argentine helicopter pilot and airlifted off the mountain. The relief and exuberance we both felt was monumental. An amazing helicopter journey to Puente Del Incas, allowed us to survey the Andes range and the distance we had climbed.

Summiting Aconcagua had given me confidence to tackle the next two – Mt Vinson in Antarctica and Mt Denali in Alaska. The greatest fear with Denali is the real threat of avalanches. There's a maze of crevasses, some 150 metres deep, just waiting to trap an unsuspecting soul. Mt Vinson also has its share of avalanches and ferocious winds, but the temperatures around Vinson are what really test the human spirit.

Temperatures of –50 °C or –58 °F are not uncommon on Vinson. When I have conquered those two, I plan to tackle Mt Everest. My cherished ambition is to summit Everest on my birthday, May 15th. To stand on the rooftop of the world and the highest peak on earth on my birthday really would be something. In attempting to summit Everest, the mind is your greatest ally. It's your mental energy that's going to provide the high spirits to continue climbing when the mountain says no.

When I do summit Everest, there's something I'd really like to do. I want to leave a portrait of George Mallory up there. My earliest inspiration and my mountaineering mentor who dared to be different. Mallory deserves to be immortalised at the pinnacle of the world. It's because of him that people like me aspire to getting there.

THE THRILLIONAIRE® PRINCIPLE

- What is your Mt Everest and quest in life?
- How do you brainstorm, re-assess and re-define yourself?
- Having reflected back on your life, do you respect yourself?

Right and below:
Rock-star dreams, Hollywood,
California, 1990

Running with the bulls, Pamplona, Spain

Above: With Bedouin friends, Morocco, Northern Africa

Below: Camping with the nomadic Masai in Africa

Above: Living in the Greek Islands

Left: Balcony view over the Mediterranean in Morocco

Below: At home in Port Douglas, North Queensland, Australia

Left: Tornado, Hill City, Kansas, USA

Below: This apocalyptic storm front spawned three tornadoes, Attica, Kansas, USA

Above: Mig 25 jet at Zuchovsky military base in Russia

Below: Sitting in the cockpit of the Mig 25

Above: Mig 25 edge-of-space flight over Russia

Above: Mig 25 cockpit view of the edge of space

Below: Mig 25 edge-of-space flight, note the curvature of the earth

Above: In zero gravity with the cosmonaut instructors

Below: In zero gravity, 'Superman'

Above: In zero gravity videotaping upside down. Above insert: In the TSF 18 centrifuge about to do a 9 g ballistic earth re-entry

Above: To my left, Yuri Gagarin's locker with mine to my right, Star City, Russia

Below: Yuri Gagarin prior to his historic spaceflight, 1961

Below: American newspaper clipping of Gagarin's space flight

The Huntsville Times

Man Enters Space

'So Close, Yet So Far,' Sighs Cape

U.S. Had Hoped For Own Launch

Soviet Officer Orbits Globe In 5-Ton Ship

Maximum Height Reached Reported As 188 Miles

Hobbs Admits 1944 Slaying

To Keep Up U.S.A. Must Run Like Hell

Praise Is Heaped On Major Gagarin

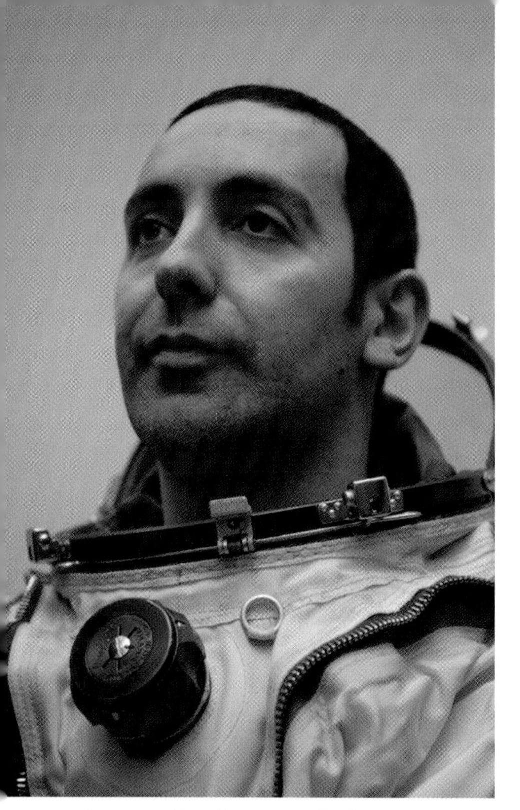

Above and right: My Sokol-KV-2 spacesuit

Below: In the Soyuz TMA cockpit during simulations

Boarding the Russian MIR submersible in the Atlantic Ocean

Above: Photoshoot and preparations before my historic *Titanic* dive

Below: Russian MIR submersible being hoisted into the Atlantic Ocean

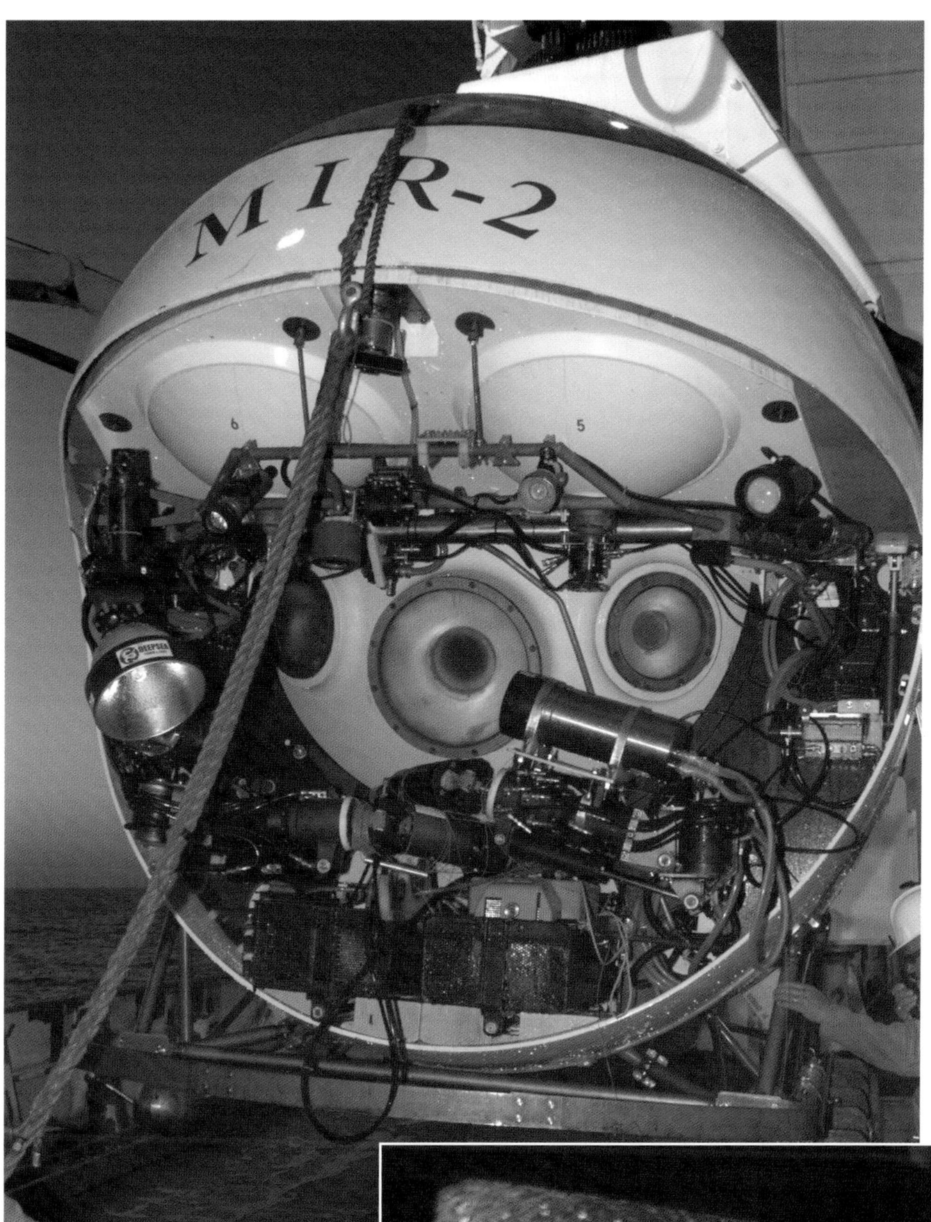

Above: The Russian MIR 2 submersible

Right: The *Titanic's* bow appears on the sonar at a depth of 13,000 ft

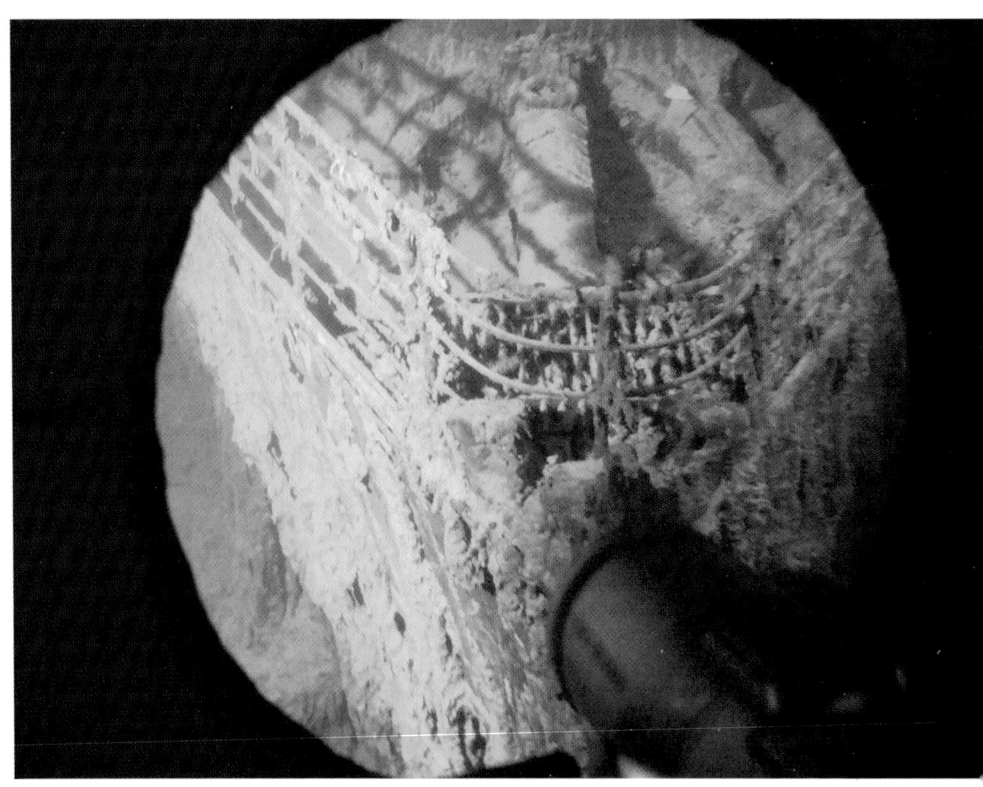

My first view of the bow of the *Titanic*

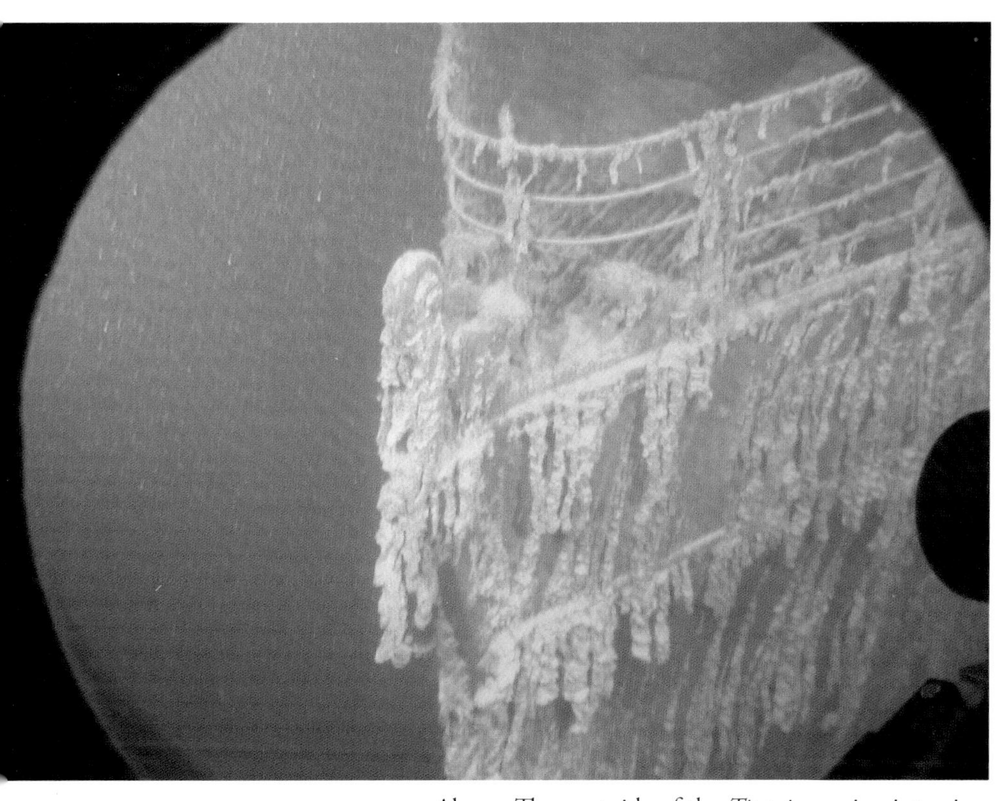

Above: The port side of the *Titanic* coming into view

Below: The Russian MIR submersible landing on the bridge of the *Titanic*

Above: Eighteen tonnes of submersible parked on the *Titanic* which has been rusting away for over ninety-three years

Below: Having lunch on the bridge section of the *Titanic*

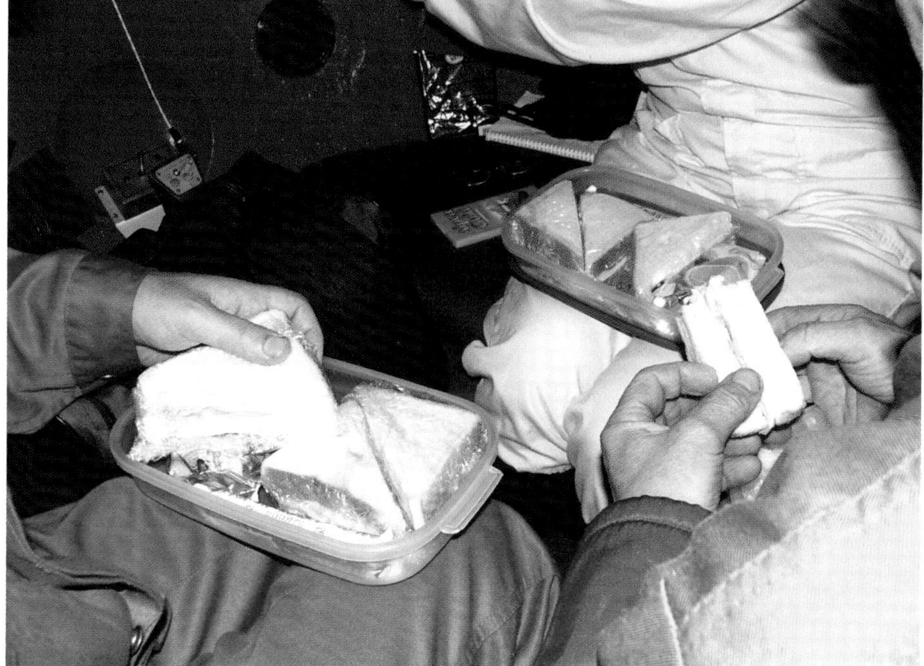

Above: Surreal view of the wreck of the *Titanic*

Above: Climbing in the Andes, South America

Below: Reaching the summit of Mt Aconcagua at 22,841 ft (6,962 m)

Above: Negotiating the penatantes above advance base camp, Argentina

Below: At 19,340 ft (5,895 m), the summit of Mt Kilimanjaro, the rooftop of Africa, Tanzania

Above: Playing golf against the backdrop of the Egyptian pyramids

Below: Private Egyptian antiquities tour

Sleeping in the King's Chamber of the Great Pyramid, Egypt

The pyramid gatekeepers who permitted me access to the King's Chamber in the Great Pyramid, Egypt

(In order to protect the identity of the gatekeepers, their faces have been blurred.)

The Financial Freedom Institute FFI Racing Car

Above: On stage at Money Masters LIVE

Below: My sister Victoria, Bob Proctor and me at Wealth Celebrities, Los Angeles, USA

Inset: Spending a white Christmas on the Antarctic Peninsula

Main picture: Adventure Odyssey® expeditions in Antarctica

Above and below: The International Space Station (courtesy NASA)

Opposite page: Earthrise from the moon (courtesy NASA)

The ultimate goal of walking on the lunar surface (courtesy NASA)

Chapter 10

Money and the education factory

The real voyage of discovery consists not in seeing new landscapes but in having new eyes – Marcel Proust

I HAVE SPECIFIC CONTROVERSIAL VIEWS REGARDING the academic world that most of us have undertaken in life. One of those controversial views is the concept and relevancy of the education provided to us. So what is education? My concept of education is as follows – an individual should learn how to speak, read and write in their own chosen language, and simply seek specialised knowledge. There are two paths to knowledge and education. One is general, the other is specialised. General knowledge, no matter how great in quantity or variety it may be, is of but little use in the accumulation of wisdom and monetary gain. General knowledge is the knowledge you have of facts or irrelevant material that will not furnish your life. Specialised knowledge is intellectual wealth. Used with the correct ingredients, it has the ability to provide you with a prolific and rewarding life.

From a teaching perspective, a PhD is an academic degree of the highest level. The term *doctorate* comes from the Latin *doctor*, meaning 'teacher'. It originated in medieval Europe as a licence to teach at a university. Most university professors specialise in teaching theoretical knowledge. They certainly do not specialise in the organisation, or the use of any particular knowledge. Knowledge will not attract prosperity, unless it is diligently organised and intelligently directed.

I personally do not have any tertiary qualifications or letters after my name, only numbers after my name. Proven, practical principles that I adopted, had manifested the accumulation of wealth in my life and the raising of my financial thermostat. Most people tend to set their financial thermostats for generating thousands, not millions of dollars. Others set their financial thermostats for generating hundreds, and not even thousands. There are some individuals who have set their financial thermostats below zero. They have been frozen in time and they don't know why.

Specialised knowledge is a specific, astute and savvy insight into the subjects that are relevant to the prosperity of your life. Once you define this specialised knowledge, you become a player and not a spectator. Education is power, but the application of it is paramount. Any subject that is going to lead you towards achieving your goals is a specialised subject that I advocate.

A lack of understanding of this fact has been the source of confusion to millions of ignorant individuals who falsely believe that 'knowledge is power'. Knowledge is only potential power. The application of specialised knowledge reigns supreme. This 'missing link' in the antiquated academic systems of education known to civilisation today, may be found in the failure of educational institutions to educate their students how to harness their collective thoughts and apply their acquired knowledge.

Let's examine the word 'education'. That word is derived from the Latin word 'educo', meaning to educe, to draw out or to develop from within. An educated individual is not one who has an abundance of general knowledge. An educated individual is one who has so developed the faculties of their mind that they may acquire anything imaginable without violating the rights of others.

Let's examine the case of Henry Ford. Henry Ford was the founder of the Ford Motor Company and father of modern assembly lines used in mass production. Many people make the mistake of assuming that, because Henry Ford had but little 'schooling,' he was not a man of 'education.' During World War One, a Chicago newspaper published certain editorials in which, among other statements, Henry Ford was labelled as ignorant and uneducated. Mr Ford objected to the statements, and brought suit against the paper for libelling him. When the suit was tried in the courts, the attorneys for the newspaper pleaded justification, and placed Henry Ford, himself, on the witness stand, for the purpose of proving to the jury that he was ignorant and uneducated. Mr Ford was asked questions such as the following:

'Who was Benedict Arnold?'

'How many soldiers did the British send over to America to put down the Rebellion of 1776?'

In answer to the last question, Mr Ford replied:

'I do not know the exact number of soldiers the British sent over, but I have heard that it was a considerably larger number than ever went back.'

Finally, Mr Ford became tired of this line of questioning, and in reply to a particularly offensive question, he leaned over, pointed his finger at the lawyer who had asked the question, and said:

'If I should really want to answer the foolish question you have just asked, or any of the other questions you have been asking me, let me remind you that I have a row of electric push-buttons on my desk, and by pushing the right button, I can summon to my aid men who can answer any question I desire to ask concerning the business to which I am devoting most of my efforts. Now, will you kindly tell me, why I should clutter up my mind with general knowledge, for the purpose of being able to answer questions, when I have men around me who can supply any knowledge I require?'

That answer floored the lawyer as there was excellent logic to the reply. Every person in the courtroom realised it was the answer, not of an ignorant man, but of a man of real education. Any individual is educated when they know how to acquire it and how to organise that knowledge into definite plans of action. Through the assistance of his 'Master Mind' group, Henry Ford had at his command all the specialised knowledge he needed to enable him to become one of the wealthiest men in America.

In all my years of enlightening global clients regarding the concept and creation of money, almost every adult would tell me, 'If only I had been taught about money, and the discipline and accountability of it, my life would have turned out differently.' You wouldn't believe how often I hear that remark regarding the failures of the academic schooling system. The broad subjects that are taught are often fairy floss for the mind. There are not enough concrete paradigms to nurture the mind into allowing it to think – to question, to probe. Paradigm paralysis and stagnation is the result. In order to reaffirm the definitive caution of money, we need to understand the relationship of it. Money should be your obedient diligent servant or nothing at all. Money is the servant, we are the masters and this equation should never be reversed. As Bob Proctor once told me, 'The most basic law governing true financial success is to always love people and use money, rather than the reverse.'

To really understand money, and to make it your servant, you need to change the money code. As mentioned before, money should be your obedient, diligent servant – or it should be nothing at all. Money must work for you, rather than you working for money. What you need to do is to change the polarity of how you relate to money.

When most people think of money, they feel a negative vibration – they think fearfully of debt, and what they owe, and how the money just seems to slip through their fingers. Think about how you regard the visit to the letterbox, with the fear of receiving bills in the mail. What are your real feelings at this stage? Where are you with regards to money? Are you the servant or the master?

The majority of my global clients seeking financial freedom are 'baby boomers', the post-war age group who were born between 1945 and 1965. In those years, following World War Two, the countries of the United Kingdom, United States, Canada and Australia experienced an unusual spike in birth rates, a phenomenon commonly known as the 'baby boom'. If they were only exposed to the Mind and Wealth Prosperity concepts and distinctions of my education as teenagers, their lives could have turned out differently. Life for some is a misery of linking more pain to money than pleasure. They wish somebody had taken them aside and blessed them with some form of fiscal education. Baby boomers globally were sold the dream of going to school, volunteering to go out into the world, acquiring a job that they did not particularly like and work really hard for forty years. The instructions were to work Monday to Friday, maybe Saturday to pay bills and taxes. Then at age sixty-five they would retire. Within a few years whilst struggling to service their lifestyle, they would exit this world and fertilise daffodils.

Any individuals struggling through life in miserable jobs have digested the program of the system to the point where it encompasses their being. In today's modern age we have a new phenomenon, 'terra incognita', a Latin phrase used to describe unknown land. Those employed in a job are in unknown territory and in a dire unpredictable predicament. Job insecurity will be standard protocol. Job insecurity is now officially one month's notice if you are paid monthly, and one week's notice if you are paid weekly. Can they turn their lives around? Yes, they can. Any life can be turned around. Firstly, it takes massive action. You must also raise your level of awareness and understand that the only difference between living in a rut and in a grave is the dimensions. In terms of financial freedom, it's never too late – or too early. A few years ago, I had a client come to me who was ninety-five years of age. I thought, wow, a paradigm pioneer at that age.

My youngest client thus far has been a young child from Singapore who was fiscally educated by me when she was nine. It's never too late or too early for anyone to embrace positive change and empowerment. I am simply the pilot in their transformation. I encourage clients to search for ways they can serve other people. This will ensure they lead a fulfilling life by becoming an outstanding example for others to follow.

A relationship with money is imperative. One of the formative lessons I provide to young teenagers is a philosophy I adopted with great success. My wallet philosophy consists of keeping notes only and discarding coins. This means that I refuse to pocket small change of whatever denomination. Collecting change from any transaction, be it a restaurant, retailer or supermarket will only energise emotions of scarcity in later life. If you remove yourself from collecting the small change and focusing on the larger notes, you will integrate a higher consciousness of prosperity. Put back the small change into circulation and do not accept it. If you reside in a country where you have one dollar or two dollar coins, then collect those coins and deposit them into a money box for a charitable Christmas donation at the end of the year. Clients have used my philosophies and find that during the festive season of Christmas, they have collected over $300 in coins which they use to purchase gifts for underprivileged children. The laws that dictate this prosperity thinking suggest that you visit a child in a hospital with the least amount of visitors. The philosophies can also be applied to adults. I personally carry a minimum of $1,000 dollars in a money clip at all times. We need to come from a space of abundance. Often you see adults with only $5.00 or $20.00 in their wallets or purses which really resonates scarcity. At all times we must feel abundant and exuberant in order to transcend our life to the highest order.

With regards to the current education regime, personally I don't think the academic situation provides a solid financial foundation for life. Without a foundation, teenagers are already dipping their toes into financial quicksand. As they become submerged in that quicksand, their thinking becomes far less exuberant. The educational school system guarantees one thing. It will provide you with a job, one single source of 'time traded for money' styled income and the role of a future taxpayer. The educational school system is a factory assembly plant for the purpose of producing taxpayers. I personally favour a self-tutored, purpose-designed approach to education as opposed to sending kids to school. This will ensure a well-rounded, cosmopolitan education with specialised knowledge.

If you haven't been fiscally educated about money, you're gambling. As teenagers mature into adulthood, plagued by the lack of cash flow in their lives, some gamble on slot machines, horse racing or play the lottery for that one in fifty-three million chance of winning. Assuming they win the lottery, the same individuals often have less money within two years than they had before they won. Such a vast amount comes their way – and they blow it within two years through indiscriminate purchases and the accumulation of fiscal liabilities and spending habits. They never possessed a financial formula to attract money into their life in the first instance.

Let me share an inspirational story with you, a metaphor which was a catalyst for my personal educational growth and my very own paradigm shift.

> Once upon a time a very strong woodcutter asked for a job in a timber mill, and he got it. The pay was really good and so were the work conditions. For that reason, the woodcutter was determined to do his best. His boss gave him an axe and showed him the area where he was supposed to work. The first week, the woodcutter cut down eighteen trees. 'Congratulations,' the boss said. 'Continue going that way!'
>
> Very motivated by hearing the boss's words, the woodcutter tried harder the next week, but he only could bring fifteen trees. The third week he tried even harder, but he could only cut down ten trees. Week after week he was cutting down fewer and fewer trees. 'I must be losing my strength', the woodcutter thought. He went to the boss and apologised, saying that he could not understand what was going on. 'When was the last time you took time out to sharpen your axe?' the wise boss asked.
>
> 'Sharpen my axe? I had no time to sharpen my axe. I have been too busy trying to cut trees …'
>
> The next week after learning this valuable lesson from his boss the woodcutter went and did a joint venture with a chainsaw company and was able to broker a deal with the timber mill where he made a percentage of the increased profit as a result of any productivity increases. Armed with his new education and strategies he was able to cut down 180 trees a week and retired in just seven months.

In life we go to work on auto-pilot, year after year. We then become so institutionalised, that we lose our faculty of thinking, become a warehouse of facts and retire broke. All because we simply never educated or sharpened our financial minds. A valued education is one which stimulates our minds and provides the leverage to catapult it without restraints.

Kids are like sponges. They embrace concepts with ease and their absorption rate is high. They have not been disillusioned or embraced negative financial habits. This is the age where the formula to success and prosperity requires a high degree of discipline in order for them to chart their own road.

Kids normally operate on 100,000 energy cycles per second, questioning everything they do and the instructions they have been provided with. This is an 'awareness state' where they question and challenge and never assume. As maturing adults our energy cycles become contracted and restricted to only 20,000 energy cycles which is very similar to a 'herd-type' comatose institutionalised state. We lose that faculty of thinking aspect and become more statement orientated. We justify ourselves with 'excusitis' and become defensive. Hence we fail to challenge the environment surrounding us. If you are in a 'low energy state', what do you think happens to your health? Sadly, you leave yourself vulnerable and open to disease. Disease is another word for disharmony, when your body is not at ease and not resonating in harmony. This is the critical time where you need to rewire your unconscious state.

Our minds also have the capacity to operate on 200,000 cycles per second, also known as the 'mastery state'. At 200,000 cycles per second our focus is laser targeted with an abundance of energy. This is the critical thinking phase that produces those halogen moments of certainty in your life. After churning through data from our unconscious state this energy cycle produces the most pivotal changes in thought and in most cases, an enlightened and profound change of thinking.

Let me walk you through the energy process here. Our nervous system receives millions of bits of important sensory data about the events that are transpiring around us. We interpret this information via our five senses. Visually (sight), auditory (hearing), kinaesthetic (feeling and touch), olfactory (smelling) and gustatory (tasting). Our mind filters and catalogues the information. Our mind filter will also delete certain data to stop us from being bombarded. When our body is completely at ease or in 'deep sleep mode', alarm bells are set off when your mind has finished the sensory download.

This phase of thinking occurs most often during your sleeping hours. Have you ever noticed when you wake up out of a deep sleep in the middle of the night for no reason feeling incredibly alive and beaming with energy? What do most people do? They force themselves to go back to sleep. Why? They are programmed to think that they should be asleep at that time and to wake up in more conventional hours. So by choosing to go back to sleep, how do you normally feel when you wake up hours later? Most people feel tired and drained in energy. Why is this? Did you know that this high energy cycle of the 'mastery state' is what inspires and provides us with new paradigm shifts. When we fail to exploit this opportunity our mind will punish us. 'If you abuse your mind, your mind will reciprocate with interest'. You must record your ideas at this moment and make the conscious decision to not go back to sleep. My greatest transformations have occurred at this 'mastery state'.

At eighteen, young adults should ventilate their lives, explore their dreams, aspirations and energise what sparks their imagination. The benefit and wisdom of travel is the ultimate life education. The experiences you have and the characters you meet forge your new identity and insights within your life. As you experience historical locations, you are constantly being challenged to assess your understanding of things. Rarely do you come back from a trip the same person as before you left.

The grim reality of life is that most young people attend secondary or high school, than automatically attend college or university. Some may abandon their university plans after studying two or three years, often disillusioned and enrol into the workforce. The chance to go overseas has disappeared. By travelling you will find out what you want to do, what you represent, and you'll be able to define what you want to achieve. In short, you'll come to understand your 'why' factor. You will be able to decipher the answers to all the looming questions plaguing your mind. This process will awaken your sense of purpose. You will provide sustenance to the legacy of your life and be remembered by future generations as opposed to being a forgotten face. You will draw strength as opposed to being a drain on those around you. You will become an illuminating inspiring force for others to follow. When you travel, immerse yourself with someone who is like-minded, who is also seeking inspiration in their life. Experiencing new cultures will only mature your mindset. Integrate yourselves into the country that you're in. Don't be a spectator – be part of it and assimilate. Your obsessive desire to acquire the ancient principles of enlightened living will elevate and transcend you to your chosen path. Your vision will become clear only when you can look into your heart, because who looks inside, awakens. Who looks outside, dreams. By jettisoning any part of the past, which no longer contains fuel for the journey and which has in fact become excess baggage in your life, you reinvent and redefine your boundaries.

With all the new paradigms and educational discoveries, none of these invaluable qualities can be indefinitely sustained without a steady diet of prosperity consciousness and conditioning. It is the personal responsibility of each of us to demand the very best from ourselves. There's no question that positive vibrations can provide that needed external spark to reset our internal circuits for twenty-four hour 'Positive Power and Performance'. A daily dose of motivation assists us in coping with the challenges we face every day, giving us strength and reinforcing our beliefs in our own abilities. A well-balanced daily infusion of motivation can help lift our spirits, restore our confidence and ignite our creative energy just when we need it the most. With these principles, we go beyond and raise our level of awareness to inspire others with a pulse, regarding our vision. It's an old maxim, but it's true: everyone has a fascinating story to tell. We are the result of every decision we make in our lives. Today is the first day of the rest of OUR lives!

THE THRILLIONAIRE® PRINCIPLE

- What is your concept of education?
- On what setting have you set your financial thermostat?
- In regards to your relationship with money, are you the master or the obedient diligent servant?

Chapter 11

Tornado storm chasing

Where the heart is willing, it will find a thousand ways. Where it is unwilling, it will find a thousand excuses – Arlen Price

WHETHER IT'S A MIGHTY RIVER BILLOWING OVER A WATERFALL and plunging into a gorge, or the blood-curdling roar of a volcano ruminating deep within, the forces of nature can be both fearful and breath-taking. Nature has many faces. We are all charmed by its spell-binding beauty – the colours of the rainbow, the symmetry of a spider's web, the millions of ways in which mother nature weaves her magic. But the forces of nature are also incredibly powerful. When unleashed, they can act with devastating fury and consume everything in their path. The power of nature is captivating.

It might sound dangerous, but I'd like to be in the eye of a storm, to feel the energy, and to experience the might of nature's rage. I imagine hurricanes to be a gigantic blur of wind and rain and things rushing by. To observe one would be spectacular, but I suspect it wouldn't be as memorable as witnessing a tornado. What intrigues me about tornadoes is that mankind doesn't know a whole lot about them. They are formed by the confluence of a myriad of factors, and they come together in a sideshow of pulsating energy, eerie sounds and explosive fireworks. Tornadoes are nature's orchestras. They can be horrendously destructive, but they are so complex that they're almost mystical.

A tornado is a violently rotating column of air which is in contact with cumulus clouds. Cumulus clouds are clouds that are usually of a puffy, popcorn-like appearance, with noticeable vertical development and clearly defined edges. They can be found singly, or in lines or clusters. Tornadoes come in many sizes, but are typically in the form of visible condensation funnels, with the narrow end touching the earth. Often, a cloud of debris encircles the lower portion of the funnel.

Most tornadoes have wind speeds of 110 miles per hour – about 175 kilometres per hour – or less, are approximately 250 feet (about 80 metres) across, and travel several kilometres before dissipating. However, some tornadoes attain wind speeds of more than 300 miles per hour – about 480 kilometres per hour – and stretch more than a kilometre across, and stay on the ground for more than 100 kilometres. The Fujita Scale is used to rate the intensity of a tornado by examining the damage caused by the tornado after it has passed over a man-made structure. The Fujita scale ranks a tornado from an F1, being a moderate tornado to an F5, being an incredibly devastating tornado.

There have been some amazing eyewitness accounts of tornadoes. One is from a man and woman who took refuge under a bridge and watched a semi-trailer get caught in a twister in 'tornado alley', the American Midwest belt famous for its tornadoes. The truckie in his semi-trailer got swallowed up into an F3 tornado, rotated four or five times in the vortex and was sucked 500 metres into the air. Eventually, the tornado spat the truck out and it came crashing to earth. Don't ask me how, but the driver survived. The brutish thrust of tornadoes is witnessed every May in that stretch of the American heartland encompassing Oklahoma, Nebraska, Kansas and the Texas Panhandle.

In May 2007 I went to experience the tornado season. I arrived in Oklahoma City on May 14th – five days after an F5 tornado had ripped through the south-west Kansas town of Greensburgh and destroyed it. Twelve people died. Nearly all the town vanished, leaving just two houses standing. It was one of the most ferocious twisters ever to hit tornado alley. I personally travelled through Greensburgh a fortnight after the catastrophe, and what was left of the town still resembled a war zone. There were Black Hawk helicopters and military police still present to warn off looters. Throughout tornado alley, there were collection points asking citizens to donate funds to the townsfolk of Greensburgh, most of whom lost everything. Because the premiums are so high, many home owners in tornado alley cannot afford insurance against tornado damage. When all they own is in their house or farm, they lose everything. The tornado hit Greensburgh at 7 pm on May 9th, and Greensburgh had no warning of it. Nature gave no indication to meteorologists. What we do know most certainly is that tornadoes are most likely to occur between 3 pm and 9 pm.

Storm chasers perform a storm-spotting service to communities by predicting where tornadoes may form, and therefore assist the authorities to help householders prepare.

Most houses in tornado alley have shelters. In the old days, shelters might have been out in the backyard. Now many are under the carpet in the lounge room. Folks hear the warning siren, roll up the rug and head down into the concrete shelter to sit the storm out.

For my ten days of storm-chasing, I teamed up with Jack Kertzie, a meteorologist and highly-experienced storm-chasing friend of mine. Storm chasers discuss the respective merits of hurricanes versus tornadoes in the same manner that motor buffs might argue about their favourite automobile brands. When we met in Oklahoma, Jack told me he chases tornadoes every May and hurricanes every June and July.

He said he had survived three hurricanes, including Hurricane Katrina which devastated New Orleans. 'Dude, they're boring,' he scoffed. 'They're just big storms. Man, there's an art to tornado chasing'.

For Jack, the science of chasing tornadoes or, more precisely, being close to where a tornado is likely to form, is a strategic exercise requiring experience, analysis and a cool head. It's a game of chess using motor vehicles, driving hundreds of kilometres to put yourself in a position that is close enough to see the action but not so close that you become part of it. It's a game of probabilities. Because I trade the stock market as one of my multiple streams and pillars of income, which is essentially a business of financial probabilities, the science of locating tornadoes really appeals to the analyst in me. As for the thrill-seeker in me, well, chasing tornadoes is one adventure I just had to embrace. Jack was happy to have me along. He loves friends coming out with him. He told me that most people think he's crazy, so he's happy when someone else shares his obsession.

I arranged to spend ten days with Jack. On the first morning we went through all his satellite gear. I was keenly interested to discover everything about tornadoes – not just the adrenalin rush of the chase. Jack taught me how to read satellite maps and software, what to look for, and how to identify potential storm fronts. His chase vehicle had all the equipment – satellite navigation systems, laptops and instant access to the internet. He was able to send images of a tornado from his digital video camera to the television networks within seconds of it happening. What's more, the networks would make a cash deposit in Jack's bank account within minutes of receiving his tornado pictures. When you see tornado or hurricane images on television, there's a good chance you're looking at Jack's work.

After we studied the satellite information on that first morning, Jack had a big smile on his face – he said there was good news. He pointed to a couple of major storm fronts developing from the Rocky Mountains and explained that, once they fused with the warm air from the Gulf of Mexico, there would be spectacular tornado activity within forty-eight hours. 'Have a look at these clouds' he said, pointing to a cloud mass on his satellite screen. 'These are cumulus clouds heading towards Kansas.' My curiosity about storm-chasing is as much about how tornadoes form as it is about how they unravel. I wanted to know what ingredients make such a phenomenon.

Before I joined up with Jack, I had been researching the winds, the barometric pressures and the influence that the Rocky Mountains have in the formation of tornadoes. If I was to get the most out of my tornado experience, I wanted to know everything about them. May is tornado month in the American Midwest.

Every year there are over one hundred tornadoes across tornado alley brought on by a combination of factors. First, you need the blue skies to 'cook' the ground.

Next, you need warm air currents from the Gulf of Mexico. Third, the warm air is met by the cooler air from the Rockies. When these intersect, cumulus clouds develop and wall clouds with a lowering cloud base appear.

For the storm-chaser, the art is to predict where the tornado will develop, and to drive to that position. Tornadoes usually spit out on the south-east, so it's best to remember that when you're getting into position. Over the ten days that we were together, Jack and I crossed four state lines, averaging 400 to 500 kilometres a day. Storm-chasers start early. We were up at 7 am, studying the satellite pictures, analysing where we needed to situate ourselves for the afternoon fronts. We spent about two hours getting the satellite information and plotting our route. After 9 am we set out to drive, usually for four or five hours, so we could put ourselves in the most probable position. Our first encounter was in Texas. We headed south by south-west from Oklahoma to the Texas Panhandle and the town of Amarillo. There was enough storm activity brewing that we were confident a tornado was going to strike between 3 pm and 4 pm. I realised that you have to move quickly, drive for however long it takes, get yourself into position, and be in the right place at the right time.

If you get there too late to set-up, nature won't wait. Jack's predictions were invariably accurate. As we drove down to Amarillo, we could see that the winds were already starting to pick up. The clear blue skies began to turn white, then grey, and then black. By three o'clock in the afternoon, the sky looked like pitch. When we arrived in the high probability area, we noticed an oil refinery nearby. If that had been hit, there would have been an almighty eruption. Jack's satellite warning system was giving off powerful rotational signals about a tornado building up. Circles were popping up on the screen, showing severe wind rotations. When the screen indicates two or three rotations, you need to get out of there. You're obviously way too close. When the rotations exceed 120 kilometre per hour, a potential twister could form.

On Jack's screen we could see the clouds rotating. Then the 'wall clouds' began to drop. Simultaneously, the temperature dropped about 15 °C in the space of a few seconds. At that moment, we realised we were right below a tornado formation. Jack warned me to get in the car immediately. 'It's going to drop on us' he said. 'Get the hell out of its way.' The winds grew so powerful that they blew over Jack's tripod and video camera, which he had set up hoping to take vision. 'Let's get the hell out of Dodge, man!' he yelled.

We moved the car and propped on a bitumen road ready to make a quick getaway.

Jack's rule is never park on a dirt or unmade road – the hail and rain can quickly render a sloppy road impassable, and you're trapped. As we gazed into the darkening cloud cover, we could hear air sirens from the oil refinery in the distance. Jack wasn't happy about the volatile nature of the tornado, and I didn't argue when he said we should leave the area. The last thing you want in your first encounter with a tornado is to go up in it. So, we got out of Amarillo. Rain and hail hit, and there was widespread torrential flooding, but the storm didn't reach tornado level. And, fortunately, the refinery wasn't hit.

However, that particular storm front produced some wild, spectacular electrical storms and a light show that night worth going a long way to see. When the fireworks ended, about ten o'clock at night, we went looking for somewhere to stay. Throughout the ten days, finding accommodation was always the last thing we thought of. We would crash late in the evening at some roadside motel and rise early to examine the day's possibilities. Our accommodation was usually old run-down motels. Ironically these same run down motels had free Wi-Fi internet access in all rooms, something most five-star luxury hotels do not even have in the bigger cities. I could keep in touch with my global businesses even in tornado alley.

On the second morning, Jack predicted there was going to be a severe storm front heading towards Kansas. We crossed the state line, noticing cumulus clouds to our west in their development phase. Jack told me to record the progress of the clouds every half hour. Sure enough they kept getting heavier and darker. We drove for four or five hours. Jack made the point that cities might have grown up on those plains – except for the havoc that the tornadoes wreak every May. When the early settlers came to the American Indians' tribal lands, they soon realised this area was regularly subjected to devastation by the twisters. Most of the Midwest is given over to the growing of wheat, barley and grain. Driving through the towns of Kansas and Nebraska, we would see the old cooperative mills, where farmers once loaded up their grain for it to be taken away by rail. Now the mills are abandoned.

So many towns out there are lifeless – tumbleweeds blow across the streets, like scenes from a hundred cowboy movies.

Young people have left the Midwest in their droves for the employment opportunities of the cities. In Oklahoma, the government is still giving away free land, so long as people are prepared to till the soil. The heartland belt of Oklahoma was littered with FREE LAND signs. I had flashbacks and visions of the 'Oklahoma Land Rush' of 1889. In 1889 the opening to white settlement of a choice portion of Indian territory in Oklahoma set off one of the most bizarre and chaotic episodes of town founding in world history. Home-seekers in their hundreds had gathered to seek their free parcel of unclaimed land and file it for ownership with the federal government. It seems nothing has changed in over 100 years.

The heartland is dying, and they're desperate to fill the void. Stores are left empty. Homesteads abandoned. On most corners, there's the remains of a gas station that has closed in the last ten or twenty years. The people who've stayed behind don't look all that healthy either. I saw a lot of super-sized people, sitting on their porches, with American flags draped out front and five or six rusted pick-up trucks in their front yards. It seems every farmhouse has a graveyard of rusted picks-ups, overgrown with weeds, and a couple of old dogs lazing around in the sunshine.

The system by which people are warned of approaching tornadoes is rather quaint.

In most towns the task is left to the local sheriff or mayor to sound a tornado warning siren for townsfolk to evacuate and seek refuge in their storm shelters. We would drive into a town and the sheriff would notice our satellite dish and storm-chasing equipment and pull us over. 'Hey guys, is there something we should know?' he would anxiously ask.

When locals saw our satellite dish and the meteorological information we had in our vehicles, they would start getting worried. 'Is there one on the way?' we were asked many times. 'How long do we have, our kids are still at school.' It was spooky. We felt like prophets of an impending calamity, but I guess we were at the frontline of the news. In tornado alley, the site of a storm chaser in town is reason to be concerned.

As we drove into towns, we often saw the shutters come down on windows, and women in their backyards taking the clothes off lines.

Most people in the areas prone to tornadoes had their radios tuned to weather stations. Many listened constantly to America One, the twenty-four-hour weather station.

But it was the storm chasers who were pretty much the front line of the severe weather watch. Private storm chasers alongside the DOW 3 DOPPLER trucks provided an early warning system to feed data and tornado locations to the Centre for Severe Weather Research. The DOW 3 – DOPPLER on wheels – research vehicles travel the Great Plains in the spring and summer as part of a funded storm research program at the University of Oklahoma. These DOW vehicles may look like something from alien worlds, but if you see them, don't shoot them! They're occupied by earthlings and engaged in valuable scientific research.

Meteorologists rely on weather radar to provide information on developing storms. The National Weather Service is strategically locating Doppler radars across the country which can detect air movement toward or away from the radar. Early detection of increasing rotation aloft within a thunderstorm can allow life-saving warnings to be issued before the tornado forms.

In the few years that DOWs have been around, they have earned a place in chase lore by their unique appearance and scientific contributions. Doppler on wheels is an X-band Doppler radar anchored to the bed of a flatbed truck. It is driven by trained chase crews to the nearest possible safe location to tornadoes, where it takes detailed vertical (RHI) and horizontal (PPI) readings. The DOW vehicles have made some fascinating discoveries about tornado structure and inflow jets. One recorded the highest near-surface tornadic wind speeds on record, 318 mph in the Bridge Creek Oklahoma tornado of May 3rd, 1999.

The DOW 3 DOPPLER vehicles have excellent equipment and most of the less-sophisticated storm chasers followed them to wherever they went. There were probably a dozen or fifteen separate groups chasing tornadoes, and we regularly met up in car parks alongside the DOW vehicles or stayed at the same motels. They were storm chasers like Jack, meteorologists or weather watchers, or just interested parties coming along for the ride. Every day we'd come across each other somewhere, and get to talking about what we had seen, or what footage we had captured. Often we'd all wait for a tornado in the same area, and position ourselves at different angles around where we expected a twister to strike. There was even a local storm chaser who modified his Hummer into a chase vehicle with a satellite dish protruding from it.

Another interesting vehicle was the IMAX tank. IMAX movie photographers have literally built themselves a tank which they call TIV – Tornado Intercept Vehicle – and have been seen on the Midwest roads this spring. The TIV vehicle is designed to film tornadoes and record footage of what it's really like actually inside a tornado.

This vehicle has been designed to penetrate tornadoes and to film at close quarters. The IMAX team, in making the TIV, took a Ford 450 super-duty truck and stripped it down to the engine and chassis. After hearing about that semi-trailer getting sucked 500 metres into the air, I'm not sure how they will go if they do get caught up in a twister.

Travelling the Midwest day after day, you get to understand why so many Americans are obese. All we could find to eat was junk food – sloppy, greasy burgers and fries, with overweight waitresses taking our orders. Every store seemed to be drive through style – drive through doctors, drive through drug stores and drive through food stores. It was sheer joy when we came across a supermarket, and we could buy some ham and salads, and make a simple sandwich. The storm chasers get to know their Midwest towns, and they visit some towns more often than others.

It's an odd fact that there are some towns that get continually hit by twisters and others that never get hit. Hill City, Kansas for instance gets hit a lot. That's where I witnessed my first twin tornado – two F3s – on the third day of our adventure. Jack had pinpointed the tornado formation to a place just outside Hill City Kansas and – when we got there – we couldn't see more than five metres in front of us. The rain and hail were incredibly thick. The car was getting pelted by hailstones that were larger than golf balls. Jack warned me: 'Don't get out of the car. One hit from a hailstone will split your head.'

So, I sat in the car and captured the footage on my video camera. At another tornado encounter, near Attica, Kansas, we witnessed a truly mind-boggling incident. A twister raced across the prairie and appeared to engulf a farmhouse. Tiles started coming off the roof, sucking them up into an enormous vacuum. Suddenly, the walls started going too … and, in a couple of seconds, the whole house had vanished. We had to get out of the area and I wasn't able to return to where the house was, or to find out whether anyone had been in the house or the bunker below. They wouldn't have stood a chance in that. The year 2007 turned out to be a big tornado season. In that year 183 tornadoes touched down between Kansas, Nebraska and the north of Texas in the month of May. Tornadoes have been reported as far north as Iowa and Missouri, but the big twisters are mostly in Kansas and Oklahoma.

A few days after we left Hill City, Jack and I were in Pratt, Kansas, awaiting another severe storm front. We arrived there about 10 pm after a big day of chasing, and I turned on the local television news to see a ticker tape of tornado warnings across the TV screen, naming the towns on tornado watch that night. One of them was Pratt, where we bunked down for the night.

At around 11.30 pm after checking my emails and communicating with my business management team in London, I was feeling hungry, so I decided to walk down the road to see if I could get something to eat. I didn't take my cell phone or my camera. It was a few minutes after midnight when the street lights went out. I looked around, and the town's power grid had gone off. I was standing outside a deserted gas station, twenty minutes walk from my accommodation, and the weather started to get menacing. First there was thunder. I've seen this weather pattern before. As I gazed into the night sky, lightning joined the choreography of events. The lightning illuminated what appeared to be a vicious swirling of wind in the distance. By then, I knew a twister was on its way. With each illumination of thunder I could see a twister, maybe an F2 in size.

The temperature suddenly dropped ten or fifteen degrees. It became suddenly cold. The winds picked up. Hail started to fall – massive hailstones started smashing on to the sidewalk. I was regretting not bringing my cameras, even though I'm not sure what I could have photographed or filmed. I just wanted to record the experience.

I decided I'd risk getting pelted by hailstones and sprint back to the motel to collect my camera.

There's nothing like a looming tornado to provoke an adrenalin rush, and I'm pretty sure I've never run faster than in that dash back to the motel. I was planning on waking up Jack and the other chasers who at this stage had been asleep for at least an hour.

Unfortunately, by the time I got the camera, the moment had passed and what appeared to be a twister disappeared into the night. I went to bed that night with an uneasy feeling, thinking my motel would be hit by another storm front. I fell asleep with my laptop and TV dialled on the Tornado Weather Channel. I awoke at 6.30 am to the news that the township of Pratt did have a tornado touchdown that night just outside town. A few barns were destroyed it was reported. Yep, I experienced it alone.

For all the brute force of the tornado season, I observed some beautiful weather phenomena in those ten days and nights. I even witnessed the optical and meteorological spectrum of light of a twin set of rainbows – one rainbow piercing another. And there were cloud covers that were truly apocalyptic. The tornado alley adventure was one of the best experiences I've had. My annual pilgrimage to tornado alley has begun and the next instalment of adrenalin will continue in May next year. Getting close to tornadoes is a risk, but life is a risk. I take risks but they're calculated risks. This is a calculated gamble that I'm happy to take.

THE THRILLIONAIRE® PRINCIPLE

- Nature has many faces. Which spell-binding aspect of nature's beauty are you most fascinated with?
- What calculated risks do you take?
- What adventure theme provokes the greatest adrenalin rush for you?

Chapter 12

Multiple pillars of income

You miss 100 per cent of the shots you don't take – Wayne Gretzky

MOST PEOPLE WERE TAUGHT ABOUT FINANCES AND MONEY by their parents or relatives, who in many cases didn't make or know how to make the type of income you now only dream of. Many of us, who went on to university or college where we were programmed to simply be part of the status quo, didn't learn specific strategies and wealth accumulation principles to get us where we now want to be. And some of us were lead by advice from well-meaning friends, but think about it … do they have the lifestyle or income we desire or need? Too many friends and associates are high on advice and low on results.

When I was starting out, I would have loved to have had an investment resource and education. This particular chapter provides a unique opportunity for seriously accelerating your true financial destiny. These strategies that have the potential to fast-track your financial blueprint can be executed from anywhere globally.

Wealth is your destiny … so please, settle back in your favourite chair and discover exactly how to claim it. Take assertive command of your financial future, where money is no longer a limitation, but a potent tool you wield with power, assurance, and impact. Lao Tzu said, 'A journey of a thousand miles begins with a single step.' It is now your turn to make the decision to take that first step.

To start out we're going to read the definition of 'Wealth' taken directly from Webster's New World Dictionary. It states as follows: Wealth (welth) n. 1 Much money or property, stock market; riches. 2. A large amount [a *wealth* of ideas]. 3. Any valuable thing or things [the *wealth* of the oceans].

When it comes to investing, one single source of income is inadequate. The problem with having your income derived from one single source is that if something happens to that particular source, you will be left without any income. In order to achieve vast amounts of wealth, it is mandatory for an investor to have a multiple of income pillars and a consistent cash flow income stream. Whether it's entrepreneurial and business ventures, property investing, stock market investing, or network marketing cash flow opportunities, this secret weapon used by the wealthy elite can expedite and safeguard our finances whilst replenishing our bank balance. Can you see the value of understanding this exclusive information?

Investing requires the cultivation of the right mindset. Did you know your financial prosperity will be the average of the prosperity of your five closest friends unless you change your inner circle of influence? This one is so predictable it is amazing to the uninitiated. Take the five people who are closest to you in your life, add up their yearly income and divide it by five, to see what your annual salary will be this year. At all times we must redefine the boundaries and networks we create to ensure a high net worth and legacy for the next generation. In fact our network of associates is in direct proportion to our net worth.

As an investor we must be relaxed, logical, perceptive, and ready to tackle anything the investment world throws at us. Take a break, relax, and rejuvenate. The mind is similar to a muscle. When you go for a long run, for example, you soon run out of energy. You can't go any further. Your muscles begin to ache and you need to take a rest and recuperate before you start moving again. It's the same when it comes to being an investor with multiple pillars of income. Investing often comes down to performing in a peak performance state at a few key moments. To take advantage of these key moments, you must be relaxed. If you have strained your mental 'muscles,' you'll have difficulty taking advantage of these opportunities.

As an International Wealth Strategist, I provide cashflow solutions in generating wealth for investors. After becoming financially independent in my late twenties, I then established Financial Freedom Institute (FFI) and since that time FFI has been catapulted to the forefront of the financial education field throughout the world. I literally started a company which became a respected investor safe haven. Respect is earned and my reputation is sacred to me. I simply gain and profit emotionally when I get flooded with financially life changing success emails and letters from clients which please me on a personal level. My personal vision has always been to transform the way individuals live through education and inspiration, thereby allowing investors to discover endless opportunities to make financial freedom a reality, not a dream.

Over time, and with extensive money-mastering financial education, my clients develop perceptions and skills that will allow them to invest creatively and decisively. My financial Mind and Wealth prosperity events, in particular, *Money Masters,* is one specific example of assisting clients to develop the strategies, skills and wealth pillars ultimately designed to supercharge their investments. I developed the concept of *Money Masters* several years ago. It has since become an internationally renowned event with a truly world class ensemble of faculty speakers who educate, encourage and nurture attendees to live their dreams, make them materialise and ensure their future is mapped out and clearly defined. *Money Masters*, a global juggernaut that has already been showcased in five continents has positively affected lives across the world. The myriad of wealth pillars discussed at *Money Masters* comprise Personal Development training and the Laws of Attraction, Property Investing, Stock Market Investing, Sales Mastery, Business Entrepreneurship Training, Tax and Asset Structuring, Internet Marketing, Investor Financing, eBay and Direct Selling just to name a few. The *Money Masters* faculty of speakers consist of the most powerful and concentrated experts on mind and wealth prosperity on the planet and have collectively helped millions of people achieve astounding levels of success.

With *Money Masters* our clients' behaviours are reprogrammed, so they'll be able to unconsciously respond with their new investing instincts. Rather than following the masses, they'll intuitively act and invest independently.

And the more decisively and independently they can invest, the more profits they'll realise. We are born to evolve and harness new energies and investment opportunities. Our bank balance reflects the investment in our own financial education.

Stock market mastery

My personalised investment regime consists of Stock Market Investment, Property Investment, Property Development, Business Development, Internet Marketing, Direct Selling Opportunities and the use of Asset Protection Structures.

Regarding the stock market, my main premise is massive cash flow generation. The stock market is my engine and fuel source for real estate acquisitions. My stock market strategies are primarily designed for investors who have been thinking about high-return strategies, but don't know where to start, for investors whose traditional forms of investment are not producing the returns they want or for investors who are searching for a part-time profit-based cash flow system to produce a secondary income stream.

A unique and savvy cash flow strategy for global stock market investors is a wealth concept coined and popularised by my best selling stock market education, aptly named *Sharelord*®. *Sharelord*® has now become a leader in global education about *Renting of shares* and the *Underwriting* of stock market insurance policies and is according to our peers, one of the most highly respected educations in the world. The *Sharelord*® strategy on average has historically returned between three per cent to nine per cent per month.

The real secret of my stock market strategies is that I keep them simple, easy to duplicate and incredibly easy to understand. By removing the ego, paralysis and testosterone of the financial markets, I have managed to personally mentor and launch thousands of new investors worldwide. These same investors who would not have otherwise started to invest if it wasn't for my ability to simplify the code and language of the financial markets, have now embraced an incredible wealth pillar valid for the rest of their lives.

The unveiling of my real stock market secret is as follows. I open up the majority of my stock market positions with a credit as opposed to a debit position scenario – I generate a guaranteed income premium on my transactions up front as opposed to paying to speculate with the hope of making money. In fact, I am creating the market as opposed to really trading it. Let me share an analogy for you. On the goldfields where gold is being prospected, who really makes the money, the prospector who is the speculator on the river bed, *hoping* to strike it rich working hours and hours or the astute, educated individual who sells the pans, picks and shovels to all the prospectors who is guaranteed to get paid? Obviously the individual selling the pans and shovel creates the market and gets paid every time. In the real world of investing, ninety-five per cent of speculative investors will trade and the five per cent will create the market.

What if we were to use this analogy in the stock market! For example, global trading speculators who need to purchase option contracts to trade on the stock market need to acquire them from someone who is providing them. As a *Sharelord®*, I create the market by contracting and renting out shares to these speculators in order for them to trade them. My payout is as guaranteed as it comes. I get paid up-front rent premiums with 100 per cent certainty due to the high level of liquidity and market participants. As an example, my *Sharelord®* system of wealth generation allows an educated stock market investor to purchase shares at a wholesale rate, not retail, and to get paid a monthly cash flow rental for simply renting out their shares. Yes, you read correctly ... I said, 'Rent out shares.'

Allow me to explain. Just as a landlord rents out an investment property to a tenant, the same strategy has existed within the stock market since 1973. In this case, an educated investor will receive an income rental for simply renting out their share portfolio. But as it stands now for millions of uneducated stockholders worldwide, they will simply buy shares and maintain them devoid of any rental income. This is the equivalent to a property investor having ten or twenty investment properties and maintaining them vacant, not realising they could rent out these properties all along.

For example, assuming you bought shares that were valued at $20.00 each. If we received six per cent rental for the month per share, that would equate to $1.20 in rental premium per share. Now if we calculated the real cost of the share incorporating the rental premium, we would now have the share wholesale rate of $18.80. This means the real purchase cost of acquiring the share was $18.80, meaning we have an automatic downside buffer protecting us if the share was to drop by $1.20 in price. One of the great features of *Sharelord*® is its particular ability to offer clients the avenue to purchase stocks wholesale, not retail and the privilege of having downside protection by the percentage of rental premium received. Compare this to the average investor purchasing shares retail with no downside protection at all.

As the *Sharelord*® we give the tenant, who is the speculator, the right but not the obligation to purchase our shares. For that right, the option buyer who is the tenant of our shares is allocated a selling price for our shares, at all times chosen at our discretion. This means, we get to set the guaranteed selling price of our shares if the tenant wishes to exercise their right to buy our shares. In the event of being exercised, we simply surrender our shares over. Assuming we purchase the shares at $8.80 and rent them out at $10.00 during the month, whilst receiving $0.65 in premium, this would equate to a seven per cent rental premium. If our shares have been exercised at the $10.00 guaranteed selling price, we receive $10.00 per share and our *Sharelord*® return for the month skyrockets to twenty-one per cent. This exceptional scenario offers us a second opportunity in generating additional cashflow. If our shares are exercised we acquire new stock to rent out. If our shares are not exercised, we simply re-rent out the same shares.

My *Sharelord*® system is designed specifically for the US market and has had an incredibly profitable track record. Since eighty per cent of the world financial markets consist of the US stock market, I personally believe that every stock market investor should only trade it. My *Sharelord*® system is an excellent high leverage money maker for any investor globally. This is so lucrative, that the US government and most US retirement accounts allow the *Sharelord*® styled system of share rental to be transacted in a 401(k) plan. The 401(k) plan is a type of employer-sponsored defined contribution retirement plan in the United States, allowing an employee to select from a number of investment options in the money market investment arena.

This allows them to utilise the *Sharelord®* system in order to expedite the cash flow process and adequately make up for the years they didn't save enough for, in order to service their retirement. The *Sharelord®* proprietary formula stipulates the specific criteria of shares best for rental, at which price, which sector group and at which time frame during the rental month to achieve the highest rent.

The *Sharelord®* system, requires no more than thirty minutes per month once you have mastered it. It has the potential to be the fastest, safest, most lucrative cash flow strategy to *pay off* a home mortgage in just a few short years. It is now used by clients in Australia, New Zealand, United Kingdom, United States, Canada, Netherlands, Singapore, Barbados, Russia and Israel. *Sharelord®* has unique attributes and provides the cashflow solution to many investors problems, thus providing the ability to dismantle credit card or personal loan debt as well. In fact just recently, whilst speaking to North American investors on a Caribbean seminar cruise en route to Cozumel, Mexico and Belize, investors agreed that the powerful *Sharelord®* strategy could have significantly reduced the amount of property foreclosures. With more investors embracing *Sharelord®* as their instrumental cashflow strategy, it allows them the luxury of a cashflow buffer in the event of financial turmoil. This was evident just recently in the US where property investors struggled to service their mortgage debt with the financial institutions and defaulted on loans.

Sharelord® works in harmony with property investing and is an excellent tandem strategy. My property investments generate capital growth and my *Sharelord®* strategies provide the bonfire and cashflow fuel source to acquire more properties.

Hence by developing, what I believe to be a recession proof investing system, the additional cashflow generated can also catapult a negative geared or negative cashflow property into a positive geared property. This enables the investor to transform a liability into a valid cashflow asset investment. Doesn't it make sense to discover the income generating strategies that very few people in the world know?

Another strategy my astute global clients use is to purchase stock insurance which protects your nest egg from capital decimation, so that you can reduce risks, and sleep well at night. This is an excellent low risk strategy. Buying an insurance policy for a stock holding has been on offer to the general public since 1973, yet millions of investors have no idea of its existence. In fact utilising my *Sharelord®* principles, you have the potential to purchase stock market insurance with none of your own money – *Other People's Money*. By using a certain portion of the initial rental premium paid, a *Sharelord®* investor can use these funds to purchase an insurance policy providing further downside protection to their stock portfolio.

One of my favourite strategies is to be the underwriter of these very same insurance policies. That is, I underwrite these stock insurance policies and receive the insurance premium deposited into my trading bank account immediately. Once again, I create the market by providing a service to the individuals who buy insurance policies to protect the value of their investment. The secret to this strategy is that the majority of insurance policies expire without claim, hence providing the underwriter the ability to potentially generate thousands of dollars monthly. When you define the relationship of the insurance underwriter and the insurance policy holder, you can ascertain that the underwriter serves as the role of the bank by underwriting renewable insurance contracts. This renewable cashflow type basis strategy allows an educated investor the potential of remaining in profit mode the majority of the time.

Another strategy I love to incorporate is to control shares by using what I call a *Share Lay-By®* system of controlling shares for a fraction of the price of buying them. With this strategy, I simply lock in a buying price of shares that have been identified as to rising in price and I outlay a small deposit to secure the buying right. For example, if a stock is currently $10.00, and I believe it will soon rise in price, I take a *Share Lay-By®* on this stock at $10.00 by outlaying a very small deposit. When the stock does rise, to $15.00 for example, I exercise my right to purchase the stock at $10.00 and pay the balance of the value of the stock. This is an excellent strategy to minimise risk, initial capital and to ensure you make a guaranteed profit on the share purchase. Most investors in the financial market are not even aware of the existence of these strategies. Stockbrokers won't tell you about it, because most of them don't know either!

My stock market strategies incorporate all the features and benefits of a true dream business – no staff or customers, no age requirements, profit potential, low risk, no physical labour, trade your own hours, trade anywhere in the world, recession and depression proof, low overheads, minimal start-up capital and no complex maths or difficult-to-understand jargon. Clients who have used my strategies in the past have started trading with amounts ranging from $500 all the way up to $1 million. A recent client in the UK who embraced my *Sharelord*® system of trading is currently investing with £18 million, equivalent to $US36 million. An educated stock market investor will simply interpret these unparalleled profitable trading strategies as the most unique cash flow opportunity in decades. These are the strategies, investment formulas and specific cashflow systems that have all contributed to the explosion of millionaires across the globe.

Property investing

From a property and capital growth perspective, it is a universally held principle that if you want to retire rich on an additional passive income stream, you must invest in real estate. There is a myriad of different strategies when it comes to the wealth pillar of property investing. To capitalise on the long-term gains of property investment, it is highly recommended to never sell under any conditions.

I have utilised a specific property investing formula, and seldom have I changed my approach since 1991. Regarding residential investment properties, I select for purchase two-bedroom properties within the $300,000 to $500,000 price range. I am mainly targeting residential property in established suburbs in leafy and established residential streets within a five to seven mile radius of a major city. I prefer to invest in older period-style homes because of their scarcity and unique solid brick construction. Most of these homes have a significant land content in sought-after lifestyle locations with high rental demand by targeted quality tenants with high disposable income. The general rule is that land appreciates and buildings depreciate in value.

Older-style unique housing, circa 1890s – 1930s is a scarce product and usually a renovator's dream. It can never be built again and is ripe for rejuvenation allowing an investor to increase the equity and valuation of the property within a month. With any rejuvenation work my renovating crew undertake, I will always seek amendments to the purchase contract to allow my team to renovate during the settlement period. This will ensure I pay no interest to the financial institutions. I can immediately market the property to prospective tenants, have a guaranteed new tenant from day one of the property transfer under my control and raise the valuation and equity of the property during the settlement phase.

By raising the valuation of the property with cosmetic rejuvenation work, I obtain a new bank valuation of the property during the interest free settlement phase. This permits me to seek finance based off the new valuation price. With renovation and cosmetic work, the rule of thumb is that we invest no more than five per cent of the purchase price. This will ensure that we do not over capitalise.

With a brand new purchase of a property, most investors simply pay the retail price and the developer's profit, whilst minimising their own profit gain. The only exception to buying a new property would be is that if the property is part of an exclusive boutique development, with a secure corporate tenant in mind which will allow a long-term and leveraged rental return. The secret to investing in property is that we must purchase wholesale and ensure that the profit is in the initial purchase.

Taking a closer look at the world's emerging property markets is a great way to get on the first rung of the international property ladder. There are many locations around the world that offer something unique to invest in. Property investing in emerging markets is fast becoming an increasingly popular investment wealth pillar for many cashed up investors, whether it may be investing in Morocco, Greek Islands, Brazil, Montenegro or St Lucia in the Caribbean. With regards to the platform of overseas property investing as an additional leveraged wealth pillar, we must not limit and restrict our thinking to property investment in our own respective country. Factors to take into consideration when contemplating an offshore property investment include the following: finance accessibility, investment infrastructure, political stability, economic stability, currency, tourism and foreign ownership laws.

Brazil for example, is a major investment property hotspot. This beautiful country offers more than just stunning beaches. Brazilian property is attracting land and property investors who seek to purchase from the start and reap great rewards from both the commercial and residential sector. Cape Verde, off the coast of Africa offers a unique chance for investors to invest at the first stage of what's sure to be one of the world's major tourist resorts. Foreign property investors in South Africa are taking advantage of the economic expansion, increased international tourism and the growing middle class which is fuelling the strong demand for more holiday properties.

Morocco, the next turbo-charged capital growth frontier is just fourteen kilometres across the water from Spain, and is Europe's gateway to Africa. With an underground tunnel under the Strait of Gibraltar currently planned, it will connect the African continent with the European mainland for the first time in history. Property in Morocco is becoming more and more popular with very high class exclusive resorts being constructed and sold at prices that are very competitive. Property investors see Morocco as a real investment hotspot. Even the world's rich and famous are purchasing property in Morocco, not only due to the fact that it is a sound investment, but also because they can continue living in the same luxurious lifestyle in Morocco as they can enjoy in traditional locations like St Tropez or Monaco. Morocco currently offers property investors an investment vehicle in which to generate solid rental yields and excellent capital appreciation.

For many, Greece has been synonymous with crystal-blue waters, warm sunshine and happy, friendly people. With tourism accounting for fifteen per cent of Greek GDP, investors concentrate on buy-to-let and large scale hotels as vehicles to fuel safe investments within a strong tourist market. Montenegro is also an interesting property investment proposition as it positions itself for entry into the European Union.

Internet business

With regards to business, the creation of a company business can be the most rewarding wealth pillar and venture in your life. In relation to developing the ideal cash flow business model and solution providing service, great businesses understand the power of leverage, the power of the Turn-Key system and the power which comes from being able to produce extraordinary results through ordinary people. The Turn-Key revolution is about harnessing the model of a business and transforming it into a business that works independently of you. Hence you work *on the business* rather than *in the business*. The ideal business model and wealth pillar would be to incorporate an online presence to ensure maximum marketing penetration. The advent of the internet and its interconnected computer networks have paved the way for millions of smaller domestic, academic and business networks to market their services on a global scale.

The USSR's launch of Sputnik in 1957 spurred the United States to create the Advanced Research Projects Agency, known as ARPA, in February 1958 to regain a technological lead. ARPA created the Information Processing Technology Office which would later spawn the creation of the ARPANET. The ARPANET was one of the 'Eve' networks of today's internet. Since then, the internet has fast become a basic feature of modern day global civilisation.

The facts are staggering. There are currently, 1.3 billion people across the globe who use the internet with $7.1 trillion to be generated via e-commerce this year. More than 900,000 people say that eBay is their primary or secondary source of income. Another 1.9 million individuals say they supplement their income by selling on eBay, according to the latest survey. A global targeted audience of online users can assist any small business to expand from a local market to an international platform. Compared to traditional media, such as print, radio and TV, internet marketing has a relatively low cost of entry. Translating your business website to Chinese and Spanish allows you to market your services and products to an additional 300 million prospective online customers.

Internet marketing of products or services has brought many unique benefits to marketing, including low costs in distributing information and media to a global audience. Internet marketing ties together creative and technical aspects of the internet, including design, development, advertising and sales. Internet marketing methods include search engine marketing, banner display advertising, e-mail marketing, affiliate marketing, blog marketing and viral marketing.

The internet has provided the cash flow opportunity to unleash the inner entrepreneur in all of us as it permits a 24/7 online marketplace. The unique component of e-commerce is that it has the potential to be highly profitable, with higher profit margins and with less capital investment required.

Small-business owners who have extended their operations to the internet often find that it's the smartest, most productive, competitive step they've ever taken. When entrepreneurs move their operations online, they establish themselves on a level playing field with larger competitors. On the internet, even the smallest online retailer can be as attractive and as functional as the largest multi-national companies – without the need to have a physical presence on every street corner. The doors of an online business never close. By not running a 24/7/365 day operation, business owners may fail to seek leverage for their businesses and remain captive of an outdated offline business model.

Relationship marketing

Leveraged Business is Booming. We can all discover the path to residual financial freedom with an entirely new alternative income pillar deemed the most potent entrepreneurial opportunity for a lifetime of wealth prosperity. In Direct Selling – also called Relationship Marketing, this pillar of business is booming. This recession proof industry has grown steadily for the past twenty years with sales jumping over eighty per cent just in the last ten years. With over seventy million people worldwide participating in this investors' dream, Direct Selling generates over $110 billion in annual sales worldwide. Paul Zane Pilzer claimed that in the next seven years, there will be thirteen million new millionaires across the globe … the majority emerging from this powerhouse industry of Direct Selling.

This first revolutionary shift in marketing has investors on Wall Street and the Fortune 500 Companies adopting it. This is due to the high earning potential, residual income and rapid asset accumulation aspects of it. I have personally harnessed this business model with a great degree of success. Relationship Marketing has the cash flow benefits where you are continually rewarded based on your initial efforts on a residual basis throughout your life.

An investor's dream … an industry with steady annual growth, healthy cash flows and long-term prospects for global expansion – Fortune Magazine

It's the best investment I've ever made – Warren Buffet

Proven … to be a viable and rewarding source of income – Donald Trump

Direct Selling gives people the opportunity, with very low risk and very low financial commitment, to build their own income-generating asset and acquire great wealth – Robert Kiyosaki

One unique Direct Selling opportunity is *Webucation. Webucation*, the passport to prosperity, is education and knowledge delivered 100 per cent via the internet. It is a Direct Selling online opportunity that is exploding on a global level and according to Forbes Magazine, 'Internet education is the ***biggest emerging trend of the decade …*** *Webucation* is exploding across the globe!' When you combine that with the $64 billion per year personal development industry, this equates to an exponential opportunity. Welcome to the future of web business. With an infinite virtual income opportunity that is capable of making many online students incredibly wealthy, this *Webucation* wave of global proportions truly opens the doors of knowledge to anyone who seeks it.

The market for continuing *Webucation* is already much bigger than most people realise. Individuals who are already highly educated and high achievers increasingly sense that they are not keeping up with the world and their environment. Peter Drucker of Forbes Magazine puts *Webucation* into its true perspective. 'We live in an economy where knowledge, not buildings and machinery, is the chief resource and where knowledge-workers make up the biggest part of the work force.'

Webucation will herald a new age, as traditional schooling will not survive. The future is outside the traditional campus, outside the traditional classroom and distance learning is coming on rapidly. Through the dual technologies of web addresses and graphics-based browsers, the internet in just the last decade has stripped the cost of communicating ideas to the bedrock limit, the time cost of reading. This unique Direct Selling opportunity is enjoying buoyant times.

Another astute Direct Selling business in harmony with the previously mentioned *Webucation* opportunity is the current surge of the Wellness Revolution. The Wellness Revolution is surging around the globe and fulfilling the Year 2000 prediction of famed economist Paul Zane Pilzer, 'The fortunes of the new millennium will be created in the wellness industry.' In the same way that the invention of the motor car and the personal computer radically changed the world's economy, this next trillion dollar industry is being spawned right now through massive scientific breakthroughs in biology and cellular biochemistry. As an ageing population increasingly seeks to stay healthy and look good, the benefits will flow to businesses that can effectively supply products and services that deliver those answers.

It begins with helping ordinary people to enjoy a greater degree of wellness, to forever change their lifestyle and health, physically and financially. The tens of millions of baby boomers of the world are leading the quest for safe and effective anti-aging approaches ... demanding ways to maintain health and youthful good looks, to solve current problems and to prevent failing health and degenerative diseases. The Wellness arena and its nutritional science revolution relating to the role of antioxidants and phytonutrients, is gaining more traction by the day, fuelled by 10,000 baby boomers reaching age fifty every day.

Wealth pillars

In order to formulate and implement new wealth pillars we will need to create a plan of action. If you want to earn more, work less, and have a luxurious retirement, you're going to have to start creating multiple pillars of cash flow that do not require your direct involvement. Whether you're just started working or you've been running your own business for a while, the sooner you start thinking about how you are going to shift your current cash flow model to create more passive income, the sooner you can achieve personal and financial freedom. The two most basic types of income are active and passive.

The best way to think of active income is when you trade your time for dollars, or as some put it, you work for money. The number one thing that comes to mind is having a job. Basically, whether you're on salary or get paid an hourly rate, if you don't work, then you don't get paid. On the other hand, passive income is where money works for you. There is still some work involved. However, you do the work once, and then get paid over and over again on a residual basis. An example of a passive income stream is to own a business that you don't work in day to day. You've transacted the active work in setting it up and now you have managers and employees running it and you reap financial rewards. Leveraged passive incomes consist of for example, an e-Book author selling their e-Book through affiliates who promote the product, a relationship marketer who builds a network and receives commissions on the sales made or product consumed by people in their organisation or an individual who franchises their business model to other entrepreneurs.

There are many other sources and ways of generating passive income. Your goal should be to have at least three to five sources of passive income pillars in addition to your active income. Ultimately, you want to reach a point where you can live solely off your passive income streams. That is financial freedom at its best. Passive income can allow considerable amounts of money to be generated, because it involves the principle of 'leverage' and the abundance of time at your disposal. Relationship marketing for example does not involve a large capital outlay and therefore has no capital risk involved with it. Once a business of this sort has been established, the income can be residual, irrespective of whether the participant remains involved or not.

With the development of wealth pillars we must next determine our 'critical mass' to best plan for our retirement. What is critical mass? It is where the income derived from your assets and investments is enough to sustain you in the lifestyle you desire. After critical mass, you no longer require active employment. When you wake up in the morning, you can ask, 'What do I want to do today?' In order to achieve your desired annual lifetime income and be paid for simply breathing, you must determine how much your particular critical mass is.

With all wealth pillars, the appropriate tax and asset protection structures are mandatory. An astute and master wealth investor will ensure they have the highest quality tax structures available to protect their assets and legally minimise their tax. Wealth is more at risk these days and as a result, the RICH have adopted *financial Intelligence.* These intelligent financial secrets have eluded most global investors. For employees, uneducated business persons and investors, it has become a significant handicap in their pursuit of creating wealth. So the real question is – *how much of your wealth will you end up keeping if you do not adequately structure your business, property and share investment portfolios?*

Wealth matrix®

Financial Cancer versus Financial Prosperity! There are four Wealth Matrixes that comprise my investment cycle and Critical Mass phase.

The *Wealth Matrix*® consists of:

1 – Income

2 – Growth

3 – Momentum

4 – Lifestyle

Your *Income Matrix* should consist of income you receive from any current employment, relationship marketing opportunities, commissions or any pillar stream of cash flow. With these funds we then invest in the *Growth Matrix*, which includes, Property Investment, *Sharelord*® stock market strategies, offline and online business ventures. The income derived from the *Growth Matrix* is used to invest in the *Momentum Matrix*, which has more weighting and highly leveraged returns associated with it. Due to the highly leveraged nature of the *Momentum Matrix*, certain defence mechanisms will need to be incorporated in order to minimise any potential donation of investment capital. This particular class of investments allows for additional income generated to be used to service the *Lifestyle Matrix*. The *Lifestyle Matrix* is your main exit point to purchase that favourite European exotic car, the luxurious villa overseas and unforgettable getaways to the most remote regions of the world. As you can see, each subsequent matrix is responsible for the core prosperity formula of financial accountability.

Financial cancer occurs, when an individual ignores the second and third matrix: *Growth* and *Momentum*. The *Growth* and *Momentum* cycle of the *Wealth Matrix*® is the fuel to compounded cash flow generation. To ignore this integral part of the matrix is to do so at your own peril. This is financial suicide as most people tend to use the after tax dollars of the initial *Income Matrix* to service the purchasing of liabilities that depreciate in their lives. This methodology is most common and the cause of great financial discomfort. I often find that this type of individual only has one single bank account that has one income source of deposit, namely a job and several withdrawals to service their negative debt and liabilities. Hence this single bank account is raped and pillaged by several sources. To clarify the word liability: anything that moves is a liability, for example, cars and boats.

So how do we achieve financial prosperity and a multiple stream of income legacy?

Chart your own course and evolution to financial prosperity by setting up three individual bank accounts. Your first account will be nominated as the *Wealth Account*. The rule for your *Wealth Account* is that you pay yourself first. In fact, I would suggest that you pay yourself thirty per cent of your income immediately. The thirty per cent of any income pillar stream must be deposited into your *Wealth Account*. This *Wealth Account* must be set up with no debit card or withdrawal facility access. A cheque book will be your only link to this *Wealth Account* and the rules stipulate the following. The *Wealth Account* can only be used for the sole purpose of purchasing assets such as investment properties which will inevitably fuel the bonfire of financial freedom and cash flow in your life.

The ancient Babylonians alongside the river Euphrates in Mesopotamia four and a half thousand years ago laid down some mighty impressive laws in regard to wealth generation. The ancient Babylonians were an incredibly wealthy civilisation and their main theory was to pay themselves first, in order to ensure a cash flow buffer for further investment. By utilising this principle, and being disciplined about it, you can become the master of money. There are a couple of ways you can ensure that you save the thirty per cent – in fact one particular method I used with great success consisted of mailing an invoice to myself every week as a constant reminder. If you invoice yourself, you will be habitually honouring an agreement with the most qualified individual in the world, yourself. By acquiring as many assets as possible, you will ensure a foundation base of equity and capital-appreciating assets in your life. These assets will serve you for the rest of your life, as well as your children.

Your second account will be nominated as your *Operations Account.* The *Operations Account* will include the running of your corporation and business interests. Any associated running costs and taxable items comprise this segment of the master plan. Individual percentages will often vary, depending on personal income and financial statements. The percentages are up to you. The process is what's important. Your third account will be nominated as your *Debit Account*, which is linked to a debit card. Your debit card in this account will service any non-related investment and non-taxable items only.

With a new financial paradigm in life, we must overcome adversity and enjoy the greatness of the moment. Unfortunately many individuals are burdened by past negative experiences in life and are unable to raise their level of prosperity, thus continually allowing negativity to dictate their life.

Allow me to further enlighten you with a pertinent story. The financial story of Mark Twain, who was one of the most widely loved and celebrated American writers who became an icon of American culture and humour the world over.

> Mark Twain was sitting on his veranda one evening having a beer with his neighbour, who happened to be his local barber. A smartly dressed salesman called and was invited to sit and join them and make his presentation.
>
> The salesman went to great lengths to explain that he represented a business house marketing shares in a new product for a new company that was going to take the world by storm, and would make thousands, and possibly millions, for those who helped to finance the company now, by buying shares.
>
> Mark Twain chased the man off his veranda. 'Get out of here. I've been caught before with these wild share schemes. Why, just last year I bought a whole heap of X shares in a new company and within a very few months the company had folded up and I lost all my money. I will never buy shares again.'

> The man left and the barber neighbour escorted him off the premises. However the barber, who had not had a bad shares experience, was very interested in what he had heard, and invited the salesman to his place, next door, and he listened to the story again. The barber bought into the company and made millions! Mark Twain made nothing! Why? Because the company was selling a new invention called the Bell Telephone.

Mark Twain surrendered to his deductive mindset and limiting beliefs, hence passing up on a wonderful opportunity. As for Mark Twain, he remained in debt for a considerable portion of his life until his death in 1910. The lesson here for all of us is that we must replenish and invigorate our exuberance for life by continually persevering regardless of the circumstances.

Just recently, there was a one-hour interview on CNBC with Warren Buffet, the second-richest man in the world who has donated $31 billion to charity. Some very interesting aspects of his life consist of the following:

> He bought his first share market company stock at age eleven and he now regrets that he started too late.
>
> He bought a small farm at age fourteen with savings from delivering newspapers.
>
> He still lives in the same small three-bedroom house in mid-town Omaha, Nebraska that he bought after he got married fifty years ago.

His advice to young people? 'Stay away from credit cards, don't waste your money on unnecessary things and invest in yourself.' Warren Buffet went on to say, 'Money doesn't create humanity but it is humanity who created money.'

An investment and multiple wealth pillar business plan allows us to quell the emotions of fear and indecision and assist us in developing a methodical and systematic approach to succeed over time. At all times we must 'think billionaire', because 'millionaire' is not the same these days. In fact Jean Paul Getty in 1957 sadly philosophised that 'a million dollars isn't worth what it used to be'. Have complete freedom to do whatever you wish. Play the game of life by your rules. Not only that, but also every passing minute is a potential $10, $100, even $1,000 in extra profits you might have added to your bank account. And each passing minute is unrecoverable. It's gone forever! We can all discover the path to residual financial freedom with an entirely new multi-faceted income stream for a lifetime of wealth prosperity.

THE THRILLIONAIRE® PRINCIPLE

- Do you have a multiple of wealth pillars and a consistent cash flow income stream?
- Have you determined your financial prosperity, by the average of your five closest friends?
- Do you continually persevere, regardless of your financial circumstances?

Chapter 13

The birth of Adventure Odyssey®

Twenty years from now you will be more disappointed by the things that you didn't do than by the ones you did do. So throw off the bow lines. Sail away from the safe harbor. Catch the trade winds in your sails. Explore. Dream, Discover – Mark Twain

AFTER A NICE HOT SHOWER YOU RELAX INTO YOUR DECK CHAIR with hors d'oeuvres on hand and sip from a twelve-year-old malt scotch soaked in glacial ice that is one million years old … or for the more adventurous … imagine … after a day of photographing sub-Antarctic wildlife from the close proximity of your Zodiac boat, you can hear the crunch of sea ice sliding beneath you. You zip underneath the overhanging cliff of a 6,000 foot high glacier as you carefully steer your way ashore. You and your boarding party carry with you your skis, ice picks, ropes, tents, satellite phones, radios, food and a plan to scale a nearby mountain peak and meet your very own research vessel the following day.

Welcome to Adventure Odyssey®. A global adventure company dedicated to extreme holidays and thrill seeking expeditions throughout the globe. A unique feature of Adventure Odyssey® is that our expeditions incorporate educational curriculums specialising in Mind and Wealth Development, thus fulfilling specialised education and certainty in an uncertain world. With my dream of Adventure Odyssey®, I teamed up with a close friend, Peter Bland. Peter was the first Australian to have adventured to both the North and South Magnetic Poles. What makes Peter's accomplishment even more remarkable is that he completed his expedition to the North Magnetic Pole, hauling a sled 700 kilometres across the frozen Arctic Sea, twelve months after undergoing his second bout of major heart surgery. With the both of us at the helm, it was about two lives running parallel with common aspirations and similar dreams. We were both adventurers with a life quest to inspire others to undergo a voyage of self-discovery and prosperity consciousness.

Our recent Adventure Odyssey® ground-breaking experience was *CashFlow on Ice®*. With a dream team of Mind and Wealth mentors in Antarctica, the expedition succeeded in unlocking our client's full potential and manifesting the universal laws of attraction. For our inaugural Adventure Odyssey® expedition, Peter and I specifically chose the remote and pristine wilderness of the Antarctic Peninsula. The Antarctic Peninsula, with huge mountain ranges descending to the water's edge is abundant with wildlife, including seals, penguins and whales. With its unspoilt frontier, considered to be the most beautiful place on earth, Antarctica is devoid of power lines, billboards, television, telephones and highways. There are no designer coffee shops or cellular networks. When the engines of our vessels are turned off, the only sounds heard, are natural wildlife, water and the occasional thundering boom of icebergs calving. If you listen closely, you can hear your heart beating with excitement! This environment allowed our clients to best soak in the gifts of nature's intelligence.

For many people in the past, Antarctica was a remote and impossible destination – impossible to get to, impossible to afford, impossible to understand. With Adventure Odyssey® we have set the new benchmark in affordable adventure cruising in remote and exotic locations on the globe, including Antarctica with exciting and breathtaking possibilities. Embedded in our expeditions is the facilitation of Mind and Wealth Prosperity discoveries that will enable likeminded clients to be enriched with leadership empowerment and cash flow science education. Having pioneered and created history with this seminar adventure concept, we have since expanded our operations to include Arctic, African safari and Brazilian Amazonian expeditions.

With Adventure Odyssey®, we operate our very own exclusive, private and modern research ships. Our vessels are Russian polar icebreakers with Russian captains, officers and crew who are considered to be the world's leaders in icebreaker operations and experts in polar navigation. The Adventure Odyssey®

vessels are ideally suited to expedition cruising. They have an ice-strengthened hull and are the perfect vessel for polar seas.

All our Adventure Odyssey® onboard international expedition leaders and lecturers are highly knowledgeable, helpful and dedicated to the protection of the environment. Our vessels have a large bridge, optimised with open deck-viewing areas. They carry a full complement of Zodiac craft, excellent for landings and wildlife viewing opportunities in otherwise inaccessible areas. With three-star meals prepared by international chefs and an array of activities made available, Adventure Odyssey® appeals to the discerning adventurer seeking educational expeditions immersed in the exploration of exotic frontiers across the globe.

Other Adventure Odyssey® expeditions planned are *CashFlow Aurora*®, *Cashflow Amazonia*® and *CashFlow Safari*®. The *Cashflow Aurora*® expedition will voyage to the northern latitudes of the arctic polar zones in search of the natural coloured light displays of the angelic Aurora Borealis. Named after the Roman goddess of the dawn, Aurora, and the Greek name for north wind, Boreas, the Aurora Borealis is also called the northern lights, as it is only visible in the north sky from the Northern Hemisphere.

With the dazzling beauty of the Aurora Borealis, the sun gives off high-vacuum electrical discharge and ion particles that travel out into space at speeds of over 800 kilometres per second. The cloud of ion particles is actually a stream of plasma coming from the solar winds of the sun. As the solar wind interacts with the edge of the earth's magnetic field and upper atmosphere, the particles collide with the gases in the ionosphere and proceed to glow, producing an orchestra and array spectacle of purple, red, violet, green and blue auroral lights.

As we explore the northern latitudes of the arctic polar zones we then set course for the North Pole. While the South Pole lies on a continental land mass, the North Pole is located in the middle of the Arctic Ocean, amidst waters that are almost permanently covered with constantly shifting sea ice. We mount our expedition to the North Pole on a nuclear powered ice breaker from the Soviet Cold War era. Our nuclear powered ice breaker is amongst the most powerful and sophisticated research ships ever built.

On our return from the North Pole, we convene for an advanced business and entrepreneurs' conference at the Ice Hotel, situated in the village of Jukkasjärvi, 200 kilometres north of the Arctic Circle in Sweden. The Ice Hotel is a temporary hotel made up entirely of snow and sculpted blocks of ice. With a host of winter activities to choose from, such as dog sledding and snowmobiling, this unique destination is in a class of its own.

The *Cashflow Amazonia*® expedition explores the heart of Amazonia. The Amazon rainforest, whose ecosystem is known as the *Floresta Amazôni,* still remains the most remote and unspoiled terrestrial wonderland in the world. It is a moist broadleaf forest in the Amazon Basin of South America, encompassing seven million square kilometres (1.2 billion acres). As we venture up the least inhabited river in the Amazon Basin and explore some of the most untouched rainforest, our expedition vessel with the assistance of our rainforest guides and accomplished naturalists will explore areas very rarely visited.

Cashflow Amazonia® is the most sophisticated expedition offered in the entire Amazon region. As we venture into the heart of the rainforest we step into a time machine in the depths of a rainforest that has not changed in over a million years. Our guides are accomplished naturalists and we see creatures almost never seen by other visitors. Stopping for a spot of piranha fishing, or an evening of caiman-spotting, or trekking through the jungle searching for medicinal flora and fauna, bird-eating spiders, or even encounter a local tribe of natives, this is truly a journey of a lifetime.

The *CashFlow Safari*® expedition consists of climbing to the summit of Mt Kilimanjaro in Tanzania. Mt Kilimanjaro is the tallest free-standing mountain in the world, rising up to 19,340 feet and providing a dramatic view of the surrounding plains. The mountain's towering snow-covered peak rises majestically from the fertile green foothills of the rainforest basin. As we descend to the base of the mountain after a successful summit on the rooftop of Africa, can you imagine anything more incredible than the silent experience of floating in a balloon at dawn over the panoramic expanse of the Serengeti Plains. The Serengeti is a 60,000 square kilometre savannah which lies over Tanzania and contains several national parks and game reserves. As the sun rises over the Masai kopjes, our hot air balloon and its enthralled passengers also rises over the Serengeti. Floating in whichever direction the wind dictates, our balloon can cruise at various altitudes to allow close scrutiny of the animals below us, and to provide breathtaking long-distance views. On occasions our balloon rises to clear a tree canopy and riverine forest.

Now at treetop height, we pass directly over a vultures' nest and float silently over the Seronera River. Hippos snort and yawn, we view giraffe, wildebeests and buffalo in their natural habitat from an entirely new perspective. Eventually, we land in the wild plains of the Serengeti and are congratulated by the ground crew with a toast of champagne! We are then treated to an authentic Serengeti breakfast, prepared and served in the wild, while zebra and gazelle pass nearby.

We next venture off to the Virunga Mountains of Rwanda, in the Volcanoes National Park, for the most exciting and exhilarating wildlife experience of a lifetime, where you'll spend an afternoon with silverback mountain gorillas face-to-face and eye-to-eye. An incredible, humbling, yet up-lifting encounter you'll never forget.

We then set sail to the exotic island paradise of Zanzibar in the Indian Ocean, off the coast of Tanzania. With its tranquil, warm tropical waters and miles of beautiful sandy beaches we discover Zanzibar's old world charm and enchanted magical past. Zanzibar serves as the venue for our annual *Mind, Money, Body and Soul* conference designed to revitalise your mind, cleanse your body and energise your spirit.

Next we venture down to South Africa to transform everyday adventure seekers into underwater *explorers*. Join us as we board our state of the art shark-diving vessel for a few days' encounter with the ocean's ultimate predator, *Carcharodon carcharia,* otherwise known as the Great White Shark. Sharks are quite possibly the world's most feared animals and no doubt the most evolved predators in the ocean. Row upon row of teeth, capable of sensing the blood of an injured animal from over a mile away, it's not surprising that they are the most feared creature beneath the waves. What we are offering to clients is the opportunity to dive and meet a Great White Shark, face-to-face in the industry's largest shark cages – an encounter with this most misunderstood creature which should be more respected than feared.

Another expedition already in its advanced planning stages is the Frontiers Leaders Expedition. This journey of a lifetime will help hand-picked young people develop into the next generation of global leaders. By exposing these young leaders to Antarctica, the Frontiers Leaders Expedition, with all its magnificence and challenges will empower our next inspiring achievers with knowledge, insights and wisdom.

The goal of the Frontiers Leaders Expedition is to enhance the skills of these already exceptional young men and women to create an innovative entrepreneurial and responsible global leadership group. By recognising the importance of harnessing the rich resource of these young explorers, they can be moulded into leaders who can capitalise on the great untapped potential of their respective countries. This will enable them to lead with confidence into a vibrant and brilliant future.

From the secluded natural havens for the ultimate in peace and solitude, today's adventure travellers want so much more than a destination, they want an experience that can help them reconnect to their lives. Away from the stress and pressure from everyday life, Adventure Odyssey® has refined and perfected a genuinely unique experience about reconnecting with the important things in life. To discover a place like no other and forget for a while the real world they've left behind.

THE THRILLIONAIRE® PRINCIPLE

- When was the last time you did something for the very first time?
- Have you reconnected to the most important things in your life?
- Do you consider yourself to be an inspiring achiever empowered with knowledge, insights, new paradigms and wisdom?

Chapter 14

Sleeping with giants

People who study others are wise, but those who study themselves are enlightened
– Anonymous

MY NATURAL CURIOSITY AND CREATIVE SPARK TO INVIGORATE THE MINd and soul provided me with an unforgettable experience just recently in ancient Egypt. The reality and power of self-examination and my obsessive desire to be enchanted by the ancient principles of enlightenment enabled me to sleep alone with the giants of history, in the King's Chamber of the Great Pyramid of Giza. This 5,000 year old grand supreme and most ancient treasured antiquity of Egypt was to become my residence for the night. Even more remarkable was the fact that with Egypt experiencing over ten million visitors each year visiting the Pyramids of Giza, this was the first time in many decades that a foreigner such as myself would be privileged to sleep in the pyramid and be a part of history. The giants of history who preceded me, who also spent time in the King's Chamber of the Great Pyramid of Giza, consisted of Napoleon Bonaparte, Alexander the Great, Herodotus and Sir Isaac Newton. I myself was personally drawn to this ancient structure in search of answers about my own life, astral passage and whether there was an afterlife.

The Great Pyramid of Giza is the oldest and largest of the three pyramids in the Giza Necropolis of ancient Memphis, bordering what is now Cairo. It is also the only remaining member of the Seven Wonders of the World. It is believed to have been built as a tomb for Fourth dynasty Egyptian pharaoh

Khufu and constructed over a thirty-year period concluding around 2,560 BC. The tallest structure in the world for over 3,800 years, it is sometimes called Khufu's Pyramid or the Pyramid of Khufu.

It is situated on a plateau on the edge of the desert and marks the zenith of pyramid-building in both size and quality. The Great pyramid of Giza is composed of two and a half million blocks of limestone, each weighing two to seventy tonnes. You could build thirty Empire State Buildings with its masonry. The base of the pyramid covers thirteen acres – about five hectares – and it has a volume of ninety million cubic feet or about three million cubic metres. It is large enough to contain the European cathedrals of Florence, Milan, St Peters, Westminster Abbey and St Paul's. It is 454 feet – about 140 metres – high, equivalent to a forty-eight-story building. Construction of the great pyramids of Giza was no accident: whoever built them knew what they were doing. The Great Pyramid of the Giza plateau still emanates great mystique and seems destined to continue for ages to come.

The Great Pyramid was originally encased in highly polished, smooth white limestone and capped, according to legend, by a perfect pyramid of black stone, probably onyx. In 1356, following an earthquake that levelled Cairo, the Arabs robbed the pyramid of its beautiful casing of stones to rebuild mosques and fortresses in the city. As the stones were cut into smaller pieces and reshaped, all traces of ancient inscriptions were removed from them. A great library of ageless wisdom was forever lost.

How the Great Pyramid was built is a question that may never be answered. Herodotus, an ancient Greek philosopher believed that it would have taken over 100,000 slaves to build it. Others believe extraterrestrials built and deserted the pyramids. The sides of the pyramid are lined up almost exactly with the cardinal points of the compass and the accuracy of this alignment is extraordinary. The Great Pyramid of Giza has functioned as an enormous sundial. Its shadow to the north, and its reflected sunlight to the south, accurately marked the annual dates of both the solstices and the equinoxes.

According to our present knowledge the Great Pyramid is mostly solid mass. It's only known interior spaces being the Descending Passage (the original entrance), the Ascending Passage, the Grand Gallery, a mysterious grotto, an equally mysterious subterranean chamber, and the two main chambers. These two chambers, called the King's Chamber and the Queen's Chamber. The King's Chamber is 10.46 metres east to west by 5.23 metres north to south by 5.81 metres high. The King's Chamber is built of enormous blocks of solid red granite weighing as much as fifty tonnes. These were most likely transported by a still-unknown means from the quarries of Aswan 600 miles to the south. Within the chamber, in the western end, sits a large, lidless sarcophagus (7.5 feet by 3.25 feet) of dark black granite estimated to weigh more than three tonnes.

Throughout history, many well-known individuals and great leaders were fascinated by the Great Pyramid. They were conquerors, generals, scholars, scientists, historians and explorers. One of the most famous visitors to the great pyramid was Napoleon Bonaparte. When Napoleon invaded Egypt in 1798, he was spellbound when he beheld the fantastic structure. Napoleon expressed his pride saying, '*Soldats! Du haut de ces Pyramides, forty siecles nous contemplent.*' Translated it means, 'Soldiers! From the top of these Pyramids, forty centuries are looking at us.' His military expedition to Egypt in 1798 was not only military but archaeological as well. He took with him engineers, surveyors, astronomers, artists and archaeologists. They surveyed, measured, explored, and made drawings of the Great Pyramid.

There is an interesting real-life account about Napoleon on his visit to the Great Pyramid. He asked to be left alone in the King's chamber. When he emerged, it was reported that he looked visibly shaken. When an aide asked him if he had witnessed anything mysterious, he replied that he had no comment, and that he never wanted the incident mentioned again. Years later, when he was on his deathbed, a close friend asked him what really happened in the King's Chamber. He was about to tell him and stopped. Then he shook his head and said, 'No, what's the use. You'd never believe me.' Before taking the secret to his grave, Napoleon in his final hours hinted that he was given some vision of his destiny during his stay in the King's Chamber.

Alexander III of Macedon (356–323 BC), better known as Alexander the Great, spent several months in Egypt as part of his ongoing campaign against the mighty Persian Empire of Darius III. Alexander the Great was drawn to the Great Pyramid and also spent time alone in the King's Chamber like many famous people throughout history. Sir Isaac Newton was extremely interested in the King's Chamber of the Great Pyramid and even wrote a dissertation on it.

There is no common denominator. People from different cultures, walks of life, diverse time periods, rich or poor, great or small, have been drawn to the Great Pyramid. What draws these individuals to this place? What are they searching for? Is it purely for scholarly reasons or is there something else that draws them to the Great Pyramid. One possibility is that people are drawn to the Great Pyramid of Giza because they are searching for answers about life. They want to know who they are, where they come from, whether there is an afterlife, whether there is a God. Many are drawn to the Great Pyramid because of their interest in its architecture, mathematics, astral passage and astronomical alignment. Connections with Atlantis, aliens, and ancient astrology have all been enthusiastically suggested in numerous journals.

Almost every religion extols the virtues of meditation, from the Christian and Buddhist to the transcendental form. It is the power of the ultimate source of the Universe, cleansing our minds and souls and allowing our bodies to function at a level, which is in tune with the inner harmony and peace that has been achieved through the experience. The importance of harmony as a means of uniting the body, mind and soul to the universal source of harmony can never be ignored. The Great Pyramid, the high priest and chamber for meditation has been found to accelerate and enhance the effects and benefits of reducing the level of stress and tension in the human body, heightening one's charge of psychic energy. The Great Pyramid remains the key to the mysteries of astral projection and the truth of life after death.

Few people have actually been allowed to spend the night alone in the King's Chamber. Indeed under the present Egyptian government it is strictly forbidden. Those who have historically gained access, passed the night in the inner sanctum with varying results. It depends of course, on one's 'frame of mind' as to the effect it has. Some individuals recalled being terrified and had to withdraw from the King's Chamber experience. Certain individuals have had the most hallucinatory dreams of inexplicable beauty or complete terror. Others have experienced past lives and others have been privileged for their soul to leave the body and wander the Astral Plane.

With this knowledge in mind, I remained in awe and in total fascination of the cosmic forces of the King's Chamber and the Great Pyramid. On my recent visit to Egypt, after repeated requests, I was introduced to some very influential gatekeepers and custodians of the greatest antiquity in the modern world, the Great Pyramid of Giza. This magical introduction allowed me to radiate an abundance of vitality and energy to soak in the gift of a higher force and intelligence. It was also an experience that produced an unlikely paranormal event that by chance, could provide me the vision to my future and personal legacy. My enthusiasm was only heightened by my readings of the last recorded real-life account of Dr Paul Brunton (1898–1981).

In 1934, Dr Paul Brunton became one of the last people ever to legally spend a night in the King's Chamber inside the Great Pyramid, the eternal colossal oasis of enlightenment. Brunton was one of the first people in the modern era to take an active interest in the mystical side of ancient Egypt and its monuments. He was a British philosopher, mystic, and traveller who left a successful journalistic career to pursue his own spiritual quest, living among yogis, mystics, holy men, studying various Eastern and Western esoteric teachings. In his book *A Search in Secret Egypt*, he describes how, when travelling in Egypt in the 1930s he resolved to spend a night alone in the King's Chamber inside the Great Pyramid. Brunton planned to sit awake and alert for twelve hours in the King's Chamber, while the slow darkness moved across the African world. However, he met with problems when asking for permission from the Egyptian government. After being sent back and forth between the Egyptian Department of Antiquities and the Police Department he finally secured written permission for his eccentric request from the Commandant of the Cairo City Police.

So, early one evening he reported to the Mena Police station, signed a book which made the police solely responsible for his safety until the following day, and was led to the pyramid by a police constable, who gave instructions to the armed guard outside the building. Brunton was then locked inside the structure with an iron grill. He would be one of the last foreigners to ever get permission to spend the night inside Egypt's most famous monument. Once inside Brunton made his way slowly through the galleries to the King's Chamber.

He waited in the total silence and darkness, as remote from the outside world as if he were on the moon. Hours passed slowly by and in the increasing cold of the chamber, Brunton began to feel that there were paranormal hostile forces around him. Eerie shadows crowded in on him from all sides and a dark apparition advanced menacingly towards him. All the legends of evil ghosts haunting the areas around the pyramids told to him by Arab villagers came to his mind. Soon there was a circle of antagonistic beings surrounding him, 'monstrous elemental creations, evil horrors of the underworld' as he described them. Despite being seized by panic, Brunton resisted the temptation to turn on the flashlight and decided to see it through. It was this determination that saved him. The elementals disappeared quite suddenly, and all was dark and quiet again. Soon afterwards phantoms of a different aspect appeared – benevolent beings in the ceremonial dress of ancient Egyptian high priests. The ancient apparitions led him through secret passages within the Pyramid to a Hall of Learning, equating to a mystical journey within the mind.

This mystical experience also involved an astral projection. Brunton describes feeling paralysed, his own spirit leaving his physical body and going to the *regions beyond death*. He felt as if he were passing upwards through a narrow hole, also described in shamanic tradition and becoming a pure mental being with a sense of existence many times more vivid than when in his physical body. He described gazing down on his prone lifeless form and noted a train of faint silvery light projecting itself from his spiritual to his physical body. This account is mentioned by many people who have experienced astral projection. Brunton was given various information by his ancient guides, including the fact that the pyramid was built in the time of Atlantis, and that the pyramid's secret chambers and ancient records were all contained within the structure itself.

Then suddenly a wall opened and a priest stepped out and took him down a long tunnel. There he met his deceased family members. He heard the words of one of the priests. The priest was asking Brunton why he had come and if the world of mortals wasn't enough for him. Brunton answered, 'No, that cannot be'. The priest replied, 'The way of dream will draw thee far from the fold of reason. Some have gone upon it – and come back. Turn now, whilst there is yet time and follow the path appointed for mortal feet.'. Brunton insisted, however, that he must stay. The priest who had spoken to him then turned and disappeared. The other priest requested that Brunton lie upon the coffer. Suddenly a force came over him. In a few seconds he was hovering outside his body. He was in another dimension of less stress and strain. He could see a silver lustre connecting his new body with the one lying on the coffer. He became aware of a feeling of freedom.

Later, he found himself with the second priest who told Brunton that he must return with a message: 'Know, my son, that in this ancient Temple lies the lost record of the early races of man and of the Covenant which they made with the Creator through the first of His great prophets. Know, too, that chosen men were brought here of old to be shown this Covenant that they might return to their fellows and keep the secret alive. Take back with thee the warning that when men foresake their Creator and look on their fellows with hate, as with the princes of Atlantis, in whose time this pyramid was built, they are destroyed by the weight of their own iniquity, even as the people of Atlantis were destroyed.'

As the priest finished speaking, Brunton suddenly found himself back in his own body. He felt it to be cumbersome compared to the one he had recently inhabited. He got up, put on his jacket and checked his watch. It was exactly midnight, the hour that is customarily associated with psychic happenings! He returned to normal consciousness quite suddenly, convinced that he had undergone some kind of initiation ceremony.

Paul Brunton was one of the last foreigners to legally sleep in the King's Chamber. But perhaps, on that strange night in the King's Chamber all those years ago, Brunton came closer to finding the true secret of the Great Pyramid than anyone else.

After exhaustive networking and negotiations, by far the most wonderful thing my Egyptian minders and gatekeepers had arranged for me, was to allow me to spend the night alone in the King's Chamber of the Great Pyramid. I was determined to gain overnight access to the King's Chamber to seek my own private answers in complete darkness and solitude. After going through the antiquities bureaucratic hierarchy and after much indecision on their behalf and repeated phone calls from me, I was finally granted permission. The event kept being put off night after night until my final night in Egypt. Now this was a risky affair as it was illegal at the time and required just the right configuration of guards, that is, the configuration of guards meant that my minders had selected key trusted personnel and slipped the guardians of the pyramid the necessary *baksheesh* cash donations. For me, I was relentless in my pursuit to pass the night in the inner sanctum with the giants of history who preceded me. With the agreed passage came the unconditional agreement that I would never reveal the identity of the men responsible for campaigning and accommodating my requests.

Just after midnight on a cold night in Cairo, I was secretly escorted to the foot of the Great Pyramid by an entourage of armed guards, pyramid gatekeepers and minders. As they unlocked the gates at the main entrance of the pyramid, I was quickly ushered in to avoid any unnecessary attention. From there I made my way alone to the King's Chamber where I was left for the night. I advised the gatekeepers to keep the lights on for the first thirty minutes in order for me to orientate myself. Soon after that, the lights were turned out plunging me into the darkest dark I have ever experienced. Then, the metal doors clanged shut and I was entirely on my own. Armed only with my belief system, a one litre bottle of water and head lamp, I allowed myself to enter a receptive frame of mind to experience whatever phenomenon existed in the pyramid.

The first few hours of darkness were incredibly surreal. I pressed my body against the chamber's ancient walls. The reverberation and acoustics were mesmerising. As a musician, no recording studio or production house could capture the same ambient effect. My regret at the time was I did not have my twelve-string guitar with me to perform a few songs. The darkness and ambience of the chamber was peculiar. Like Dr Paul Brunton, I resisted the temptation to turn on my headlamp and decided to see it through the night.

The greatest concentration of energy and heat I felt, was located in the King's Chamber. This was obviously the geometric centre of the pyramid, located at one-third up its height from its base. The King's Chamber acted as an amplifier of my thoughts and energy. Every focus of thought or idea that I was manifesting into my life was amplified accordingly, with vibrant colours and sounds. With eyes shut, even attempting to clear my thoughts, I felt my body entering into a deeper state of focus and tranquil peace much more rapidly and effortlessly. I can honestly claim that a supernatural source of power or energy was present. The humidity was intense considering the freezing cold temperature outside the pyramid. Soon I felt the low drone of my breathing reverberating within the chamber and vacuum of space.

It was at this moment that I started to chant melodies to gauge a potential response from any entity within the chamber. While voicing harmonic and melodic passages to channel any psychic faculties, I could sense something in the air. An unknown presence could be felt and a friendly air came alive in the chamber. Was this aura of mystique my spiritual awakening: that my home is not the body, but the soul? I continued to chant and with more gusto I entered the nearby sarcophagus in the chamber and crossed my arms over my chest. If ever there was a time for my vulnerability to be exploited, this was it. Soon I felt numb and disconnected. It was as if I had no control on any bodily movements. I lost all reference to time and could not decipher how much time had since passed. My breathing became irregular and my low drone had dropped even lower in pitch. A low buzzing type sound could be heard, layered within the frequency of my breathing. These were my last detached imprints of internal memory and a great void seemed to engulf me.

To this day I cannot recall whether this hypnotic trance was induced upon initially entering the chamber or upon my actual positioning in the sarcophagus. I was finally awoken by the internal lights of the pyramids being illuminated. The gatekeepers were sounding the muted alarm to inform me to make haste and vacate the pyramid. Upon awakening, I felt incredibly at peace and struggled to come to grips or even attempt to summarise the events unfolding. As I climbed down the chambers shaft to the Grand Gallery I recorded my final video. I exited the Great Pyramid just after 6.00 am and thanked the gatekeepers. Within minutes, I was quietly ushered into a waiting private car and instructed my driver to take me to the international airport to make my 8.50 am flight to Heathrow in the UK.

Having recorded short videos from within the King's Chamber throughout the night, upon playback of the final recorded video, I was horrified as to the contents of it. The playback was to plague my mind. Upon closer scrutiny, there was a scene in this final video where I was recounting the awakening phase and footage of me exiting the chamber when a strange reptilian type sound enveloped the audio. I had full battery charge and memory space in my digital camera at the time of recording, yet this inexplicable mysterious buzzing type reptilian sound defied logic and anything deemed to be normal. I was questioning my belief system as to whether I was experiencing an astral 'out of body' experience as I was listening to it.

Moments into my flight from Cairo to London, I became astutely aware that a metaphysical change had indeed occurred with my being. Being an individual ever so reliant upon my ability to voice direction for others, I had literally been 'cut off at the throat.' The initiations within the pyramid had relieved me of my voice for forty-eight hours.

A few days later, whilst making passage from London to Buenos Aires en route to Antarctica for Christmas and New Year, I was sent a text message to contact a mysterious stranger who was a Shaman living in London. I was informed that there was a part of me that had been put through an initiation in the pyramid! There was a powerful energy source from beyond the portal, beyond the multiplexes, universes that was signifying a time for new beginnings and a birthing into a higher aspect of divinity. I was informed that the Shaman could shed light as to my current metaphysical predicament and provide some answers. Struggling to come to terms with the situation, I made contact with the Shaman who could channel energies.

The Shaman provided insight that in my first life, I was the first born and only son of Hermes Trismegistus, the thrice great sage. Thrice, because he was master of Astronomy, Alchemy and Philosophy. Hermes lived around 4,000 years BC in ancient Egypt. Hermes, apparently was my guide and when the time was right I would be coming home to my true self in this life.

Being New Year's Day, the Shaman told me that it was the best day for me to know who I really was and what was happening to me would now be revealed. The Shaman told me,

> Nik, the boy in you is leaving. Hermes wants you to know that he is very proud of you. Your karma is paid. You are transforming. You feel it, you feel yourself waking up, coming alive. Things taste better, sound better. And that this is just the beginning. Nothing is coincidence, all is design. You are a blessed pawn of the divine. Three is the key, Three is alchemy, Three is synchronicity. See the threes, follow the signs. Enjoy the realisations coming back through time.

Attempting to make sense of it all, I contemplated for a few hours as to the real meaning of the conversation. And with this fascinating insight and mesmerising set of events, my call with the Shaman concluded.

The recorded video footage within the pyramid still remains an enigma and biocosmic curiosity for me. History is full of phenomena which may have been caused by biocosmic energy. Examples are the Egyptian Mummies, the Biblical Ark of the Covenant and the story of Methuselah, who lived for 969 years. Biocosmic energy is the very essence of life force itself, this energy has been known to exist but, until now, no one has been able to isolate it. The Great Pyramid of Giza, the sacred seventh wonder of the world, is at last revealed to the world for its true purpose, a very powerful source of biocosmic energy. The word pyramid itself reveals its most hidden secret. Pyramid means quite literally, 'fire in the middle'. The pyramid being an accumulation of energy inside also radiates energy off the points and top. This would also have added considerably to the pyramid's storehouse of power and energy.

A Czechoslovakian radio engineer by the name of Karel Drbal also performed experiments himself with models of pyramids. He concluded that, 'there is a definite relationship between the shape of the space inside the Pyramid, and the physical, chemical and biological processes going on inside that space.' Drbal also considered that the pyramidical shape may also be responsible for the accumulation of electromagnetic waves or cosmic rays, or of some unknown energy.

Many mystical and esoteric teachings continually refer to the idea that Atlantean knowledge and records are hidden within secret chambers still to be discovered in the Great Pyramid of Giza. Atlantis really did exist, as a place, as a continent in Plato's book, *Critias*. According to Plato, the secrets of these chambers will be opened by people who are deemed worthy of being entrusted with all this sacred and spiritual knowledge.

THE THRILLIONAIRE® PRINCIPLE

- What lessons from ancient history could you embrace?
- Which biocosmic energy forces do you subscribe to?
- The importance of harmony as a means of uniting the body, mind and soul to the universal source of harmony can never be ignored. Are you currently calibrating on the same frequency of your mind, body and soul?

Chapter 15

Soyuz TMA 13 Mission

The best way to predict your future is to create it – Anonymous

SINCE THE DAWN OF CIVILISATION, SPACE HAS BEEN THE SOURCE of humanity's collective fascination – a culmination of our greatest fears, dreams, desires, and hopes. This New Frontier and last bastion of true adventure has never ceased to inspire, fascinate or challenge me. In all of human history fewer than 450 people – quietly chosen, groomed and trained behind a veil of secrecy – have escaped the confines of Earth.

***** BREAKING NEWS *****

News release from Space Adventures: 24th November 2007

Space Adventures Announces the Identity of Back-up Crew Member

For the TMA–13 October 2008 Orbital Spaceflight Mission to the International Space Station

Australian entrepreneur and investment wealth strategist selected

Today, the Virginia-based space firm, Space Adventures announced the identity of the back-up crew member for the TMA-13 October 2008 orbital spaceflight mission to the International Space Station (ISS). Nik Halik of Australia has been chosen to train as the back-up crew member alongside our orbital spaceflight candidate, Richard Garriott, famed game developer and son of a former NASA astronaut, who is currently planning a mission to the International Space Station (ISS) in October.

Nik Halik became a multi-millionaire and amassed great wealth through savvy investments in property and the stock market in his late twenties. He is thirty-eight years old and resides amongst his homes in the Greek Islands, Morocco and Australia. Nik will be an active participant in Garriott's mission and be featured in a US documentary TV series.

'Through his participation as a back-up crew member, Nik will experience first-hand how our clients train for spaceflight and he, himself, will be certified as a "fully-trained cosmonaut" and will be named to an official space mission crew, a distinction that fewer than 1,000 people have ever had, but, the combined participation is a step forward in the progression of our expansion into the cosmos,' said Eric Anderson, president and CEO of Space Adventures.

'I have dreamed of flying to space ever since I was a young boy. I watched recordings of Neil Armstrong's first steps on the moon's surface and I vowed to follow,' said Nik Halik. 'The space station will be my first stop, with my eyes focused on the moon.'

'Not only is Nik a successful entrepreneur, but he is also an avid adventurer. Among his various expeditions, he was one the first Australians to dive down five miles and land on the bow of the Titanic and he will be the first civilian and private space explorer from Australia to travel to space,' added Mr Anderson.

'Nik and I have similar exploratory backgrounds and we'll have many stories to share during our time together in Star City. I look forward to training with him because not only is it meant to prepare myself for flight, but also to prepare Nik for his future flight. I definitely will be on-hand for his eventual launch to space,' said Mr Garriott.

The pathway to entry into the cosmonaut facility is complicated, and I benefited from the assistance and networking skills of some key people I had been introduced to. This is truly a unique opportunity and honour to train for an orbital training mission. The TMA–13 back up orbital mission training for the Soyuz-FG rocket and Soyuz-TMA spacecraft will allow me to become a fully flight-qualified and certified cosmonaut.

Richard Garriott, the legendary video game programmer and designer, noted as one of the PC Gamer's 'Game Gods' is training alongside me in Star City for the TMA-13 October 2008 orbital flight. He is following in the footsteps of his father, Owen Garriott, a former NASA astronaut and is set to become America's first 'second generation' astronaut. While his father joined the NASA astronaut corps and completed two space missions during his career, his son Richard is now helping to usher in another new era in manned space exploration. He is funding his own private spaceflight to Earth's only manned outpost in orbit, the International Space Station.

For every Russian manned spaceflight mission to the ISS and Earth orbit, both a primary and back-up crew are trained for the expedition. As a member of the back-up crew, I will have the opportunity to train for an actual space mission to the International Space Station alongside other government funded professional Russian cosmonauts and NASA astronauts. My main training will take place at the legendary Gagarin Cosmonaut Training Centre (GCTC) in Russia, one of the world's leading training facilities for orbital space missions. Training at the GCTC will allow me to immerse myself in the elite world of human spaceflight where the essential skills needed for living and working in space will be honed. My Back-up Orbital Training will be approximately 1,000 hours, spread over nine months, and will require me to relocate to Russia for most of 2008.

But like all true adventures, our orbital training mission will be tested in ways we could never have imagined. Our skill and strength will be scrutinised in the greatest of testing grounds – a faraway place called Star City. Star City, north-east of Moscow, is a highly sensitive military installation and Cold War era massive facility that I have visited many times. Everything at Star City is designed to prepare aspiring adventurers for survival in the most hostile environment known to man. We will be thrown into a maelstrom that will push human tolerance to the limit. This is the actual space program the Soviets created to transform average humans into supermen.

How do you survive the vacuum of near space? How do you respond, operate and continue to work under extraordinary physical pressure? The world's largest centrifuge (TSF-18) will allow us to experience the crushing forces of a rocket launch and re-entry into Earth's atmosphere. We will endure over eight times the gravitational load we normally feel on Earth. The vestibular chair tests us for how long we can tolerate vestibular disorientation before violent motion sickness sets in. Incorporated in the testing will be an edge-of-space flight on board a supersonic MIG 25 jet fighter, cruising at over three times the height of Mt Everest. Below us, the curvature of the Earth is awesomely apparent and the horizon is 1,100 kilometres across. Only the crew on the space station will be higher than us aboard the MIG 25.

We will test our mechanical skills in the neutral buoyancy chamber, as we are sent underwater in the hydro-lab. Down below, we are tested on our ability to manoeuvre bulky space suits while repairing delicate sensors on a mock space station. We will also achieve 'zero-gravity' while still on Earth, a harrowing feat called the 'vomit comet ride'. The Ilyushin 76 is a specially-fitted aircraft that is used to train cosmonauts and astronauts in a weightless environment. From level flight, the plane pitches up to 45 degrees as passengers experience about twice their body weight. Then the plane glides over the top of the arch and passengers experience about thirty seconds of apparent weightlessness. To test our mental and psychological strength, we will face gruelling flight simulator challenges that will prepare us for the worst once in the Soyuz spacecraft with terrifying emergencies.

As cosmonauts in training we will work together to successfully pass these tests. Some emergencies will have fairly simple solutions. Others will require great skill and creativity, including Soyuz-TMA and ISS simulator training, manually docking the spacecraft or donning our spacesuits in thirty seconds. Other trainings include: altitude chamber training, spacecraft emergency operations,

Siberian wilderness survival operations course, psychological screening tests, similar to those given to the astronaut corps, physical fitness programs, extensive medical testing, crew pre-launch operations, space environment training and Russian language training.

The International Space Station is the largest scientific and technological endeavour ever undertaken. The ISS is a permanent laboratory in a realm where gravity, temperature and pressure can be manipulated for a variety of scientific and engineering pursuits that are impossible in ground-based laboratories. The ISS is a test bed for the emerging technologies for the future of mankind as we discover more about living and working in space. Aboard the international laboratory, crews also conduct medical research in space in order to develop new materials and processes to benefit industries on Earth.

When completed, the ISS will be 365 feet – about 110 metres – across and 290 feet or 88 metres, long, and it will weigh about 940,000 pounds – or about 430 tonnes. NASA's Constellation Program is currently developing spacecraft and launch systems for a new generation of explorers who will return to the Moon. By 2020, development of an outpost on the Moon will become a reality. Early lunar missions will be about a week long, but eventually stays on the lunar surface of the moon are expected to last about six months.

Private spaceflight is more than space tourism. It is the next generation of spaceflight. By rocketing to space as a privately funded and trained civilian astronaut, I will have the mandate to conduct activities that go beyond those available to government-funded NASA astronauts and Russian cosmonauts. I will have the ability to conduct activities of my choosing, and that could have a commercial benefit. From performing scientific research on behalf of a space agency, university or private company, to conducting educational programs with students all over the world or seeking publicity for a valid cause for humanity, I will have innovative plans to add value to my spaceflight experience. My customised mission is only bound by the imagination.

To have the potential to be one of the first 450 humans to ever reach Earth orbit, to rocket around the Earth every ninety minutes and complete a 40,233 kilometre journey with each single orbit is incredible. By viewing the Earth's surface and living in a completely weightless environment for over ten days will permit me to appreciate the true majesty of the universe and the fragility of Earth. Back-dropped by the blackness of space and Earth's horizon, the night sky will illuminate the planet, like I have never seen it before. For a Thrillionaire®, that's the most exciting possibility imaginable.

My life by design was never coincidental or luck. I have merely acted out the script of my life, a screenplay I wrote as a young child, a very long time ago. My manifested reality was the result of every decision made in my life. I dictated the course of my life and cleared any obstacles that threatened to obstruct my path of self-discovery. With the successful passing of new vantage points and heights in my quest for wisdom, my agenda and purpose became clearly defined. With the commitment to completion of each goal, I simply dialled into the channel of the next goal and passionately enthused to conquering it. At all times I made dissatisfaction work for me and refused to be complacent.

I was reminded as to how integral a core belief system was, only a few weeks ago at Star City. Yuri Gagarin, the Soviet cosmonaut and my first childhood mentor became the first human to travel into space on the April 12th, 1961 in Vostok 3KA-2. My father, in honour of Gagarin 's achievement presented me with a portrait of him that graced my bedroom wall as a young child.

During my cosmonaut training at Star City, we regularly undertake physical training sessions. The current gym at Star City has not changed much in appearance and equipment over the years and is still used by cosmonauts. In fact this was the same gym Gagarin trained at, for his history making flight into orbit in the 1960s. The gym locker room in the gym still has the locker that was used by Yuri Gagarin prior to his death. His gym locker contains his personal towels, shorts, trainers, tennis racquet and other personalised items. It remains there as a shrine to his eternal presence. His gym locker has a glass door for viewing by trainee cosmonauts such as myself. What is so unique about this is the fact that my gym locker is virtually next to Yuri Gagarin 's actual gym locker. I am incredibly honoured and privileged to be in the same space as my childhood hero whose portrait graced my bedroom wall for so long. As for the portrait of Gagarin that was given to me by my father, well the exact same portrait graces the walls of the gym locker room directly opposite my locker. Some people may call this serendipity.

As well as this revelation, I welcomed the exciting news and announcement that a copy of *The Thrillionaire®* book was going to be sent up in the next rocket launch to the International Space Station in April 2008. On board the International Space Station is a small library of suggested readings where my book *The Thrillionaire®* will permanently reside amongst other literary books for future explorers and voyagers to read in space. Dreams do indeed come true.

It is with an iron will that they embark on the most daring of all endeavours. To meet the shadowy future without fear and conquer the unknown.

– Ferdinand Magellan, circa 1520

THE THRILLIONAIRE® PRINCIPLE

- By re-writing your eulogy, what will it now say about your life?
- Are you currently moving away or towards your goals?
- What is your new awakened frontier and true adventure in life?

Chapter 16

Life force energy

You may chain my hands and shackle my feet; you may even throw me into a dark prison, but you shall not enslave my thinking because it is free – Kahlil Gibran

As I begin to reflect upon my journeys, it seems as if my life has been like a mirror. It has been projecting what I was putting into it. Perception is projection. I splashed a kaleidoscope of colours onto my life mosaic and possessed an abundance of energy. When you have energy and passion you glow. You are like a magnet that attracts the finer things in life, creating a metaphysical connection and a transferral of energy. At the start of every new day we should rise to greet this magnificent world as there is, and always will be, an abundance of opportunity surrounding us.

We all have an allotted 168 hours per week to explore life, to confirm our thoughts and to be in the presence of individuals who continually inspire us. Every day above ground is an exceptional day and with each passing event in our life, we should gain strength. With unbridled enthusiasm we should create a mastermind group and surround ourselves with high achievers who will propel us to our divine destiny.

Money also responded to the way I thought about it. In fact there was nothing advanced about making money once I simply changed the polarity as to how I related to it. Imagine treating money like manure. If you pile it in one place it stinks. But if you sprinkle it around, it will nourish your life and help it to grow to its full potential. By using a multiple of wealth pillars and income streams sprinkled around, we can then set out to build our wealth to critical mass.

Once we achieve this, we can donate and contribute back to society on a grand scale to leave a legacy behind.

The world's wealth is expanding at an increasing speed. Wealth is just a transferral of cash. Unfortunately, the biggest single obstacle that people face before managing to build wealth is leaving behind the unproductive financial habits and routines that they've developed over the years – and start believing that they are entitled to be rich. Some avoid financial education, apprehensive of any potential costs involved and choose to procrastinate. If they think education is expensive, they should weigh up the costs of ignorance. Imagine working in a job for forty years or should I say, landing a job for forty years, doing it for one year, but forty times over.

I clearly wasn't invincible and like many others, I experienced many challenges and suffered some setbacks. Whatever happened in my life was inconsequential. What mattered was my response to life's twists and turns. I believe this determines one's path of greatness in life. Champions learn from defeat. In fact, in the cradle of every mistake lie the roots of all success. With all new distinctions, we must share the gift of transformation with friends and family members.

Throughout my life, I remained my own worst critic, providing feedback to myself at all times and I opened my eyes and willingly accepted all the consequences of my actions. If we do not learn from the past we are doomed to repeat it. By cataloguing all discoveries and lessons on an unconscious level, I had created a benchmark to adhere to. In relation to the goals I set, allow me to give you the best advice ever. Write your goals on paper, see them, hear them, feel them, taste them and smell them 24/7. Only when you do this will you be able to internalise them, make imprints of them on a cellular level and manifest them.

We must also raise the bar and set new standards of excellence in everything we seek and aspire to accomplish. I recall reading how Ninja warriors trained as small children whilst jumping from a standing position. A bamboo shoot was planted for each child, who from that day on had to jump over it each day. Bamboo is the fastest growing woody plant in the world and their growth rate is measured at a few feet per day. There was no difficulty in the task at first because the shoots were only ankle high. But as the shoots grew into canes, the children were constantly stretched to new heights and excellence. The constant need to raise standards meant they ended up jumping over tall canes with surprising ease and confidence.

What would be the ultimate price if we fail to take massive action in our lives? If we remain subservient to everyone else and fail to satisfy our own selves due to lack of belief, we lose the publishing rights to our own life story and allow others to draft it. By entertaining a state or trance of disempowerment, our faculty of thinking remains contracted and we are far less enthusiastic about dismantling its boundaries. Our belief system has the ability to betray us. We are our own worst traitor. Remember this: Life will always reward decision makers.

I was not born into immediate wealth but I was born rich in human potential. I did have medical issues earlier in my childhood but I refused to be enslaved by their confines. I did not want to be treated any differently. Being sick or having an illness these days is wrongly rewarded and negates any chances of empowering someone. Society is programmed to reward sickness by presenting and gifting someone with flowers, chocolates or balloons upon news of their illness. This negative environment is not conducive to a balanced and positive lifestyle. The interesting aspect about being sick is for example, you could ask someone how many times they get sick each year. Most people tend to say, two or three times per year. What do you think happens? They do indeed get sick two or three times per year. We must eradicate specific words from our vocabulary. If you don't want to feel or experience these words, simply don't say them.

And finally to all the unsung heroes of the world, we cannot after all judge the biography of your life by the length of years you live. It can only be judged by the richness of the contents of your life. Certain birds you can't cage, their feathers are far too bright. Seagulls flock and eagles will always soar. By ensuring you pass the baton to the next generation, you now act as a neural bridge leading a chosen path of enlightenment.

In closing, I would dearly love to share a metaphor with you about our inner potential. A metaphor allows you to bypass the conscious, resistant level of your mind and connects you to the deeper levels of your emotion. This metaphor is about a magician with magical powers who sets out to enlighten individuals from a small village.

Standing on the edge of a cliff, near the top of a mountain, a mysterious stranger stood. The people from the village below had heard of this mysterious magician on the cliff top. They were intrigued and went to investigate. They heard rumours of his powers. The village leader with three others climbed up the path to the mountain. 'We've come to see the magician,' said the village leader. The magician looked at them and said, 'Come to the cliff edge and be enlightened. For you have come to witness my powers, I have also arrived to reveal yours. To have what you want you must come over to the cliff edge.' The cliff face had a 300 metre drop. The nervous villagers were petrified and slowly walked to the edge. The magician reassured them, that no harm would come to them. This provided a calming effect and allowed them to place their trust in him. He put his hands on their shoulders further relaxing them. As they relaxed he slowly took his hands off them. Silence followed for a few seconds. The villagers had no idea what was happening. The villagers looked at one another. 'Close your eyes,' said the magician. The villagers standing on the cliff edge took their last view of the valley below before closing their eyes, when suddenly the magician pushed them off the cliff. At first it was terrifying for the villagers, but then when they abandoned their fear and overcame their negativity, they realised their true power and remembered they could fly. In fact, they could fly all along! They jumped and grew their wings on the way down.

In the spirit of 'The Thrillionaire®' I encourage you to set flight on a voyage of evolution. Live with passion and dare to dream, make your life an epic extraordinary adventure.

THE THRILLIONAIRE® PRINCIPLE

- Have you connected with the deeper levels of your emotions?
- Are you the author of your own life?
- Are you raising new standards of excellence in your goals?

Testimonials

Pass on to Nik my most sincere congratulations on the most brilliant education I've ever done. I can invest with 100 times the wisdom. I'm amazed that Nik had the guts to put together an education that reveals the whole truth on how to invest properly. This truth has seemingly been a top secret to only the 10% investors who actually make money over the long term. That's it for me. Never again will I have to use a money manager, financial advisor or go off the lead of a stock broker or another investor. Thank Nik for me for giving me a skill that I can carry through the rest of my life and constantly develop and refine.

Never stop living out your dreams,

Rob Cartledge (Australia)

Hi Nik,

I just wanted to express my heartfelt thanks for a wonderful, wonderful trip to Antarctica. I've come back with so many great memories and in relaying my stories to everyone it makes me realise how crazy some of the things we did were. I got so much out of the trip and have come back with more motivation to keep pushing through beyond my comfort zone rather than parking where I have for the last couple of years. Before I left I thought I'd already achieved quite a bit with my investing but hearing you speak about all your global property acquisitions made me realise I've barely done anything so I'm much more raring to go and achieve more and more now. It was great to spend my trip with my father and see him accomplish and have a go at things I don't think he ever thought he'd do. That was fantastic. Seriously. I'm just amazed!

Bringing my family along to Antarctica has by far been my best investment yet and has made my relationships even stronger as we are now one with our future and the direction we want our future to go. Thank you soo much from the bottom of my heart. I absolutely cannot wait for the Cashflow Safari expedition, thank you once again.

Sheree B (Australia)

Dear Nik,

Thank you so much. If I'd known a year ago when I attended Money Masters London, what your education contains, I'd have borrowed, begged, done anything to get my hands on it. Anything! Thank you for your generous spirit, your striving for perfection and your superb teaching ability that assumes absolutely no preexisting knowledge. Thank you Nik for all your hard work and for your great warmth that adds so much to the Money Masters experience. With love and thanks,

Janete Sumner-Rivers (UK)

Had a fantastic time Nik. Great boost and desire to accomplish great things. I came especially from Geneva, Switzerland, for this event and my expectations have been largely met. I also met some very dynamic people."

Greg Linn (Switzerland)

It is a breakthrough in mind set that I have been waiting for – free at last, free at last, God Almighty free at last!

Andrew H (Australia)

The ah ha light went on so many times during the experience as the 'secrets' and mechanics were revealed. Now I feel like the little boy who just inherited a lolly shop.

Tony R (Australia)

I think that Money Masters is amazing, it is a wonderful experience for like minded people to come together and encourage and support each other to getting one step closer to excellence.

Azania Shaka (UK)

It's fantastic! So many mysteries, technology, shares, property – illuminated! It's an amazingly generous concept.

Sharon Foster (Ireland)

The most amazing three days. I have been committed to my own development for many years, but have experienced huge growth and knowledge which will have a big impact on my life.

Lorraine Tapper (UK)

It is a sermon of hope, a dream awakening event for anyone who really desires to become who they want to be.

Kayode Alese (US)

AWESOME! Life changing. Quitting my job Wednesday, handing in my notice. Sacking my boss!
Alice Chai (Australia)

The best weekend ever. Nik – your team, your guests, the information given, so much so great. So let's put it all together, it is a life changing event.
Cathy O'Brien (Australia)

This is definitely one of the most valuable events I have ever attended. I see my business possibilities and profitability expanding exceptionally upon implementing just a fraction of the ideas presented here.
Danny Sullivan (Australia)

Hi Nik,

Thanks a million for the Money Masters UK experience. I am very grateful for the opportunity ... and most especially the value it brought to my club members. I have been attending seminars for 10 years but none of them has ever affected my life and destiny like the Money Masters UK. Money Masters UK is causing a lot of ripples within my circle of influence. Such was the impact of it, that everybody wants to attend in the future.
Kelvin Ugbodu (UK)

Intense, very informative (a lot of info to take in, but worth it). Enjoyable, awesome logistics team. Engaging to the max! Thank you for looking after our bears on this planet that are at the mercy of cruel people and Nik, thank you for bringing my future husband, the love of my life, back home to me, instead of working so far away in such a dangerous job.
Maria A (New Zealand)

Excellent strategies for personal wealth and growth which no university can ever teach.
Eugene Y (Australia)

This would have to be the best financial event I've attended. These last 2 days have set me on a new course for my financial future – thanks Nik.
Noel R (New Zealand)

I am thrilled at Nik's education. Your assistance is unparalleled in this industry. Self-knowledge is the path to self determination and growth – my finances are now a growth industry. I am still smiling at the mention of it.
Christine W (US)

I love the energy Nik releases. He has made me realise the world is our paradise.
Steve T (Australia)

Very informative – made a black art almost understandable! I can't wait to start investing. Nik, you live and breathe this stuff – your excitement and energy is contagious!
Pauline S (Australia)

There are times in life when you realise you are at a defining moment – this is one of those moments and you have my thanks for being part of this new experience. This is where I needed to be to realise, reaffirm and recalibrate my goals.
Paul N (Australia)

Exhilarating! Nik is an exceptionally unique individual with seemingly boundless energy, enthusiasm and desire to help people help themselves – he shows the way!
Barry H (US)

Fantastic! My greatest investment to date has been the 2 days spent with Nik. The returns from this should be great and not limited to monetary returns alone. Thanks
Mark A (UK)

Awesome! For a sceptic like me, it was a revelation and I'm glad I've done it. Where has this stuff been? Where have I been? Thank's a heap Nik and team.
Brian S (Ireland)

Bloody brilliant! This will revolutionise my financial future. It has provided the tools to execute the strategies for financial freedom only previously dreamt of. It really is inspirational. The possibilities opened up by these strategies are mindblowing. It will make life far more accessible; careers, dreams, holidays, social/community contribution far more rewarding.
Kirsten O (Australia)

Index

MIND & WEALTH PROSPERITY SCHOLARSHIP

VALUED AT $15,977.00

Includes two complimentary tickets to attend any Life Masters, Money Masters and Internet Masters event anywhere in the world.

For a limited time only you have the ultimate opportunity to reward yourself ...

with the most informative, fast-paced and revolutionary Mind & Wealth Prosperity events on the globe. This exclusive invitation and complimentary scholarship may very well be the SHORT-CUT discovery you've been waiting for. The Greatest Investing, Business, Entrepreneurial and Personal Development opportunity ever imagined.

It's a celebration of networking with like-minded investors and entrepreneurs. It is an exciting opportunity to potentially alter your financial blueprint exponentially and take control of your financial future.

For more information and to secure your complimentary Mind & Wealth Prosperity Scholarship valued at $15,977.00 simply register online at

www.TheThrillionaire.com

SUCCESS